C000148632

Macmillan Computer Science Series
Consulting Editor: Professor F.H. Sumner, Un

A. Abdellatif, J. Le Bihan, M. Limame, *Oracle – A User's Guide*

S.T. Allworth and R.N. Zobel, *Introduction to Real-time Software Design, second edition*

Ian O. Angell, *High-resolution Computer Graphics Using C*

Ian O. Angell and Gareth Griffith, *High-resolution Computer Graphics Using FORTRAN 77*

Ian O. Angell and Gareth Griffith, *High-resolution Computer Graphics Using Pascal*

M. Azmoodeh, *Abstract Data Types and Algorithms, second edition*

C. Bamford and P. Curran, *Data Structures, Files and Databases*

Philip Barker, *Author Languages for CAL*

A.N. Barrett and A.L. Mackay, *Spatial Structure and the Microcomputer*

R.E. Berry, B.A.E. Meekings and M.D. Soren, *A Book on C, second edition*

P. Beynon-Davies, *Information Systems Development*

G.M. Birtwistle, *Discrete Event Modelling on Simula*

B.G. Blundell, C.N. Daskalakis, N.A.E. Heyes and T.P. Hopkins, *An Introductory Guide to Silvar Lisco and HILO Simulators*

B.G. Blundell and C.N. Daskalakis, *Using and Administering an Apollo Network*

T.B. Boffey, *Graph Theory in Operations Research*

Richard Bornat, *Understanding and Writing Compilers*

Linda E.M. Brackenbury, *Design of VLSI Systems – A Practical Introduction*

Alan Bradley, *Peripherals for Computer Systems*

G.R.Brookes and A.J. Stewart, *Introduction to occam 2 on the Transputer*

J.K. Buckle, *Software Configuration Management*

P.C. Capon and P.J. Jinks, *Compiler Engineering Using Pascal*

J.C. Cluley, *Interfacing to Microprocessors*

J.C. Cluley, *Introduction to Low Level Programming for Microprocessors*

Robert Cole, *Computer Communications, second edition*

Derek Coleman, *A Structured Programming Approach to Data*

S.M. Deen, *Fundamentals of Data Base Systems*

S.M. Deen, *Principles and Practice of Database Systems*

C. Delannoy, *Turbo Pascal Programming*

Tim Denvir, *Introduction to Discrete Mathematics for Software Engineering*

D. England et al., *A Sun User's Guide*

A.B. Fontaine and F.Barrand, *80286 and 80386 Microprocessors*

J.B. Gosling, *Design of Arithmetic Units for Digital Computers*

M.G. Hartley, M. Healey and P.G. Depledge, *Mini and Microcomputer Systems*

J.A. Hewitt and R.J. Frank, *Software Engineering in Modula-2 – An Object-oriented Approach*

Roger Hutty, *Z80 Assembly Language Programming for Students*

Roger Hutty, *COBOL 85 Programming*

Roland N. Ibbett and Nigel P. Topham, *Architecture of High Performance Computers, Volume I*

Roland N. Ibbett and Nigel P. Topham, *Architecture of High Performance Computers, Volume II*

Patrick Jaulent, *The 68000 – Hardware and Software*

P. Jaulent, L. Baticle and P. Pillot, *68020–30 Microprocessors and their Coprocessors*

J.M. King and J.P. Pardoe, *Program Design Using JSP – A Practical Introduction*

continued overleaf

E.V. Krishnamurthy, *Introductory Theory of Computer Science*
V.P. Lane, *Security of Computer Based Information Systems*
Graham Lee, *From Hardware to Software – An Introduction to Computers*
A.M. Lister and R.D. Eager, *Fundamentals of Operating Systems, fourth edition*
Elizabeth Lynch, *Understanding SQL*
Tom Manns and Michael Coleman, *Software Quality Assurance*
A. Mével and T. Guéguen, *Smalltalk-80*
R.J. Mitchell, *Microcomputer Systems Using the STE Bus*
Y. Nishinuma and R. Espesser, *UNIX – First contact*
Pim Oets, *MS-DOS and PC-DOS – A Practical Guide, second edition*
A.J. Pilavakis, *UNIX Workshop*
Christian Queinnec, *LISP*
E.J. Redfern, *Introduction to Pascal for Computational Mathematics*
Gordon Reece, *Microcomputer Modelling by Finite Differences*
W.P. Salman, O. Tisserand and B. Toulout, *FORTH*
L.E. Scales, *Introduction to Non-Linear Optimization*
Peter S. Sell, *Expert Systems – A Practical Introduction*
A.G. Sutcliffe, *Human–Computer Interface Design*
Colin J. Theaker and Graham R. Brookes, *A Practical Course on Operating Systems*
M.R. Tolhurst et al., *Open Systems Interconnection*
J-M. Trio, *8086–8088 Architecture and Programming*
A.J. Tyrrell, *COBOL from Pascal*
M.J. Usher, *Information Theory for Information Technologists*
B.S. Walker, *Understanding Microprocessors*
Colin Walls, *Programming Dedicated Microprocessors*
I.R. Wilson and A.M. Addyman, *A Practical Introduction to Pascal – with BS6192, second edition*

Non-series

Roy Anderson, *Management, Information Systems and Computers*
I.O. Angell, *Advanced Graphics with the IBM Personal Computer*
J.E. Bingham and G.W.P. Davies, *A Handbook of Systems Analysis, second edition*
J.E. Bingham and G.W.P. Davies, *Planning for Data Communications*
B.V. Cordingley and D. Chamund, *Advanced BASIC Scientific Subroutines*
N. Frude, *A Guide to SPSS/PC+*
Percy Mett, *Introduction to Computing*
Barry Thomas, *A PostScript Cookbook*

Oracle
A User's Guide

A. Abdellatif, J. Le Bihan, M. Limame

English language edition edited by Ken Deighton
Dorset Institute

MACMILLAN

Authorised English language edition of Oracle, by A. Abdellatif, J. Le Bihan and M. Limame, first published 1989 by Editions Eyrolles, 61 Boulevard Saint-Germain, 75240 Paris

Translated by M.J. Stewart

First published 1990

Published by
MACMILLAN EDUCATION LTD
Houndmills, Basingstoke, Hampshire RG21 2XS
and London
Companies and representatives
throughout the world

Typeset by
Ponting–Green Publishing Services, London

Printed in Great Britain by
Billing & Sons Ltd, Worcester

British Library Cataloguing in Publication Data
Abdellatif, A.
Oracle: a user's guide. – (MCSS)
1.   Microcomputer systems. Relational databases. Management
I.   Title   II.   Le Bihan, J.   III.   Limame, M.   IV   Deighton,
Ken   V.   Series
005.756
ISBN 0–333–54215–0

The following are registered trade marks or trade marks of Oracle Corporation:
Oracle, SQL*Calc, SQL*Connect, SQL*DBA, SQL*Forms, SQL*Graph, SQL*Menu, SQL*Net, SQL*Plus, SQL*Report, SQL*ReportWriter, SQL*Star, PL*SQL, Pro*Ada, Pro*C, Pro*Cobol, Pro*Fortran, Pro*Pascal, Pro*PL/1.

Contents

1 Introduction

1.1 Preamble

During the 1960s the first database management systems (DBMS) appeared, designed to tackle the problems of manipulating large numbers of files. These arose from inconsistencies because of data duplication in the files. The first commercial DBMSs such as IDS and IMS were able to avoid a large number of such problems.

The year 1970 is considered to be a decisive year in the database field since it was then that E.F. Codd proposed his relational model. Up until 1976, this new model had not got beyond industrial and university research laboratories. So IBM's San Jose laboratories, originators of the relational model, developed System R while the University of Berkeley produced the Ingres prototype. The following three years saw experiments with university prototypes. It was only from 1979 that the first commercial products were brought on to the relational DBMS markets, from Oracle, Ingres, etc. As for SQL/DS, IBM's first such product, this was not announced until 1982. From then on relational DBMS markets reached adulthood.

So far as distributed databases are concerned, research began around 1977. Prototypes like SDD-1, Sirius-Delta and Porel were developed in various research groups. The first commercial products offering some distributed DBMS functions only became available at the end of 1986 and the beginning of 1987. These are basically the SQL*Star from Oracle and Ingres/Star.

1.2 Aims of the book

The primary aim of this book is to give a detailed description of one of principal systems that have characterised the relational DBMS market in recent years, namely the Oracle DBMS.

The book outlines the general architecture of the system as well as the role and use of each of its components.

The readership envisaged is quite broad: from the decision maker who requires a complete overall view of the product and its functions, through to

1

the database administrator and to the applications developer.

The decision maker should find sufficient concise and complete information to place Oracle in the relational world without becoming lost in the details of design and use.

For developers, database administrators and end-users, the book will also serve as a learning manual and reference for the system.

It will also serve as a basis for teachers using the Oracle system for database courses, especially those that involve the Standard Query Language (SQL). There are simple examples given for most of the commands in order to aid comprehension.

To summarise, this book should prove a useful guide for anyone who wishes to launch into the Oracle world. All the examples that illustrate the concepts and use of Oracle have been prepared under version 5 on PC/MSDOS.

1.3 Plan of the book

The book is divided into four parts:
The first part consists of chapters 1–4 and gives a general overview of relational databases and the Oracle system.

Chapter 1 sets the historical context and describes the aims.

Chapter 2 presents the concepts of the relational model and describes the current industrial DBMS scene.

Chapter 3 gives a general presentation of how the Oracle system functions.

Chapter 4 is devoted to the basic architecture and distributed architecture of Oracle; it describes the functions and components of the Oracle layers.

The second part consists of chapters 5–9. Chapter 5 introduces the objects manipulated by SQL. It describes a database that will serve as an illustration of the various manipulations.

Chapter 6, 7 and 8 are given over to successive discussions of definition, manipulation and data control under SQL.

Chapter 9 describes Oracle's interactive interface for manipulating a database by SQL commands.

Part 3 consists of chapters 10–13. It presents the following tools:

Pro*C   : a programming interface with the C high level language
SQL*Forms   : a screen form generator integrated with Oracle
SQL*Calc   : a spreadsheet compatible with Lotus 1-2-3
SQL*Report : a report generator
SQL*Menu   : a menu generator

Part 4 deals with aspects of data administration of an Oracle database, together with extensions introduced with version 6 of the product.

2 The Relational Model

2.1 Basic principles

2.1.1 Concept of a database

A database can be defined as being an integrated set of data that models a given universe. The data used by various applications is grouped together, thus avoiding any problems resulting from duplication. A database has associated with it a schema, called a conceptual schema, that describes the structure and type of data that it contains, together possibly with some rules (or constraints) that must always be obeyed. A person responsible for the database, called the database administrator, is in charge of supervising the verification of these constraints.

The conceptual schema does not take account of the physical aspects of the data storage. It therefore gives a global picture of the database that is not always that of all the users and applications. This is why the ANSI/SPARC group introduced the three-level architecture (see figure 2.1). The internal or physical level allows the data storage to be shown, by means of an internal schema. The conceptual or global level corresponds to the conceptual schema of the database. Thirdly, the external or local level allows different users to have restricted views of the database according to their responsibilities and needs. Each user or group of users does not see the database in its totality, but only a part, currently called a view, which is defined via an external schema.

A database is managed by a database management system (DBMS) whose principal objectives are:

- the description of data
- the manipulation of data
- the maintenance of data integrity
- transaction management
- access concurrency
- security
- access control

3

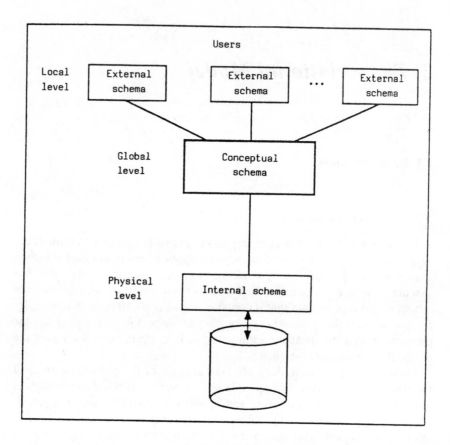

Figure 2.1 The three perception levels of a database

These functions will be described as they apply to the particular case of Oracle in the following chapters.

2.1.2 *Data models*

A database contains objects from the real world and associations between these objects. These objects and associations are represented and manipulated using a data model. There are three data models that are differentiated by their method of representing and manipulating the associations between objects.

The hierarchical model only allows one type of association to be represented, that of father and son. An object may have several sons but a son may only have one father. This model may be sufficient for some universes, but it is generally limited.

The network model allows all types of link to be represented. Its disadvantage lies in the method used to access data. To access an object the whole of the database may have to be traversed until it is found.

Finally, the relational model, based on an elaborate mathematical theory, allows the tabular representation of both objects and associations between objects. This model is characterised by the simplicity of data representation (which may be seen as a disadvantage in some cases) and the power of its operators for data manipulation. The following section will describe this model.

2.1.3 The relational model

Data structure
A relational database appears as a set of relations, hence its name. These relations are also called tables. Each relation has a schema that describes its structure and an extension that corresponds to the state of this relation at any given moment. The schema of a table is made up of a set of attributes (or columns), a subset of which constitutes the key that allows the other attributes of the relation to be identified (the schema is more usually regarded as the attributes of all the tables in the database). The values of the attributes are atomic, that is, they are indivisible, and they belong to the same domain. A domain is a set of values of the same type. Several attributes may share the same domain and can then be compared. Despite the importance of this concept, almost all the commercial relational DBMSs do not support it.

The extension of a relation is made up of a set of tuples (or lines). A tuple corresponds to a set of values taken by the attributes of a table to represent an object or a link between objects in the real world. For a given object, and at a given moment, we may not have access to the total data that describes this object. In other words, the values of some attributes may be unknown. These unknown values are called null values.

Although the manipulation of a relational database does not present great difficulties as we shall see, its initial design is not always clear. In fact, a bad translation of the real world in terms of relations may cause problems, such as data redundancy, that in turn leads to multiple updates, or the risk of incoherent data in the case of incomplete updates. Such problems are the source of abnormal behaviour in relations at times of update, hence the need for a process called the normalisation of relations. This mechanism is based chiefly on the concept of functional dependency between attributes. Design methods for relational databases have begun to be developed in recent years (for example, SECSI, REMORA, etc).

Data manipulation

To manipulate data, the relational model has a set of grouping operators, which are applied to the relations as a relational algebra. We can identify two types of operator: unary and binary. A unary operator applies to a single relation, whereas a binary operator applies to two relations. Projection and selection are the only unary operators. The binary operators are union, intersection, difference, cartesian product, join and division. The first three of these may only apply to relations of the same schema.

The selection (or restriction) of a relation consists of choosing the tuples that satisfy a given condition. The projection of a relation onto certain of its attributes only yields the columns that correspond to these attributes. The union of two relations gives a third relation made up of all the tuples of the two relations. The intersection of two relations yields all the common tuples. The result of the difference of two relations is a set of tuples that belong exclusively to the first relation.

The cartesian product of two relations is a relation whose schema is made up of the attributes of the first and the second relation and whose lines are obtained by the juxtaposition of each line of the first relation with all the lines of the second.

The joining of two relations is only possible if these two relations share some attributes of the same domain. The joining is made according to one or more of the attributes, called join attributes. The result is a subset of the cartesian product made up of the lines that satisfy the join condition. The join condition may be an equality between the join attributes or an inequality ($<$, $<=$, $>$, $>=$ or $\neq$). In the first case, the operation is called equi-join and in the second theta-join. If the two operands of a join are identical, the operation is called auto-join (a relation joining with itself).

Finally, the division of a relation of n attributes by a second relation (sub-relation) made up of m (m $<$ n) attributes of the first relation gives a third relation having as its schema the n-m attributes that remain. These are formed from tuples whose concatenation with those of the second relation gives a tuple of the first relation.

2.2 Current state of the DBMS market

Up until 1984, the DBMS market was dominated by hierarchical and network products. These systems exhibited a lack of separation between the logical level and the physical level. As a consequence they necessitated a set of complex rules for data manipulation. The first relational DBMSs sought to solve such problems in order to facilitate greater productivity for developers and users, faster response and simpler application maintenance. But the simplicity of the relational model was not sufficiently convincing in itself. This was due in part to commercial inertia from the products already on the market and also partly to the unproven performance of relational DBMSs. In the interim, special efforts have been made to improve the performance of the latter.

Apart from improved performance, two other factors have contributed to to the proliferation of relational DBMSs: the standardisation of SQL (Standard Query Language) and the availability of a variety of tools designed for each DBMS. Before becoming an official standard, SQL was already a *de facto* standard because it is non-procedural, easy to use for developers and users and available on most systems. The developers of relational products also became interested in the ergonomic qualities of their products and in the development tools that could be used in the DBMS environment. This has given rise to the following tools and interfaces that have been made available.

Data manipulation via screen forms: Viewing and updating operations may be carried out by completing the fields in a predefined form on the screen.

Language preprocessors for data manipulation: The access commands of a database may be used by programs in the traditional high level langauges, such as C, COBOL, Pascal, PL/1, etc.

Report generators: The results of a request can be put in the form of a report with facilities for a title, header, footer, etc.

Application generators: A simple but powerful language, that is compiled or interpreted and allows an application to be developed rapidly. This is often called a fourth generation language (4GL).

These tools have enabled the application area of relational DBMSs to be broadened. They now cover areas ranging from decision applications through prototyping to transactions.

Table 2.1 shows the main relational DBMSs available on the market. It is not comprehensive and not all of the systems are purely relational.

Some of these DBMSs were designed by the manufacturer for its own range of machines. This is the case with DB2 for IBM and RDB for DEC. Others are intended to function under a particular operating system, such as Informix under Unix (although an MS-DOS version is available). Most of the other DBMSs are supported by a large range of machines and operating systems. This is especially true of Oracle and Ingres.

Table 2.1 Main commercial relational DBMSs

DBMS	DESIGNER	MAIN TOOLS
ADABAS	Software AG	NATURAL, ADASQL, NETWORK and ADANET
ADR	Applied Data Research Inc	DataQuery, DataReporter, Ideal, DL, Empire, PC DataCom, PC Peer and D-Net
DB2	IBM	ADPS, CSP, QME, AS and ECF
Empress	Rhodius Inc	SQL, M-Builder, M-Writer, Precompilers
Informix	RDS, then Informix Software Inc	ISQL, ESQL/C, 4GL, Ace, Perform
Ingres	RTI	Interactive SQL, Ingres/4GL, Ingres Menu, SQL Preprocessor, Query-By-Form, Application by Form, Ingres/Net and Ingres/Star
NonStopSQL	Tandem	SQLCI(SQL Interactive, Report Writer and utilities) and Programmable SQL
Oracle	Oracle Corporation	SQL*Plus, SQL*Forms, SQL*Report, Pro*, SQL*Calc, SQL*Graph, SQL*Net and SQL*Star
RDB	DEC	VAX Rally, VAX TeamData and precompilers
Supra	CINCOM	SPECTRA language, NORMAL, BRAID, MANTIS and programmable interfaces
Sybase	Sybase Inc	TRANSACT-SQL, VQL, Reports, Data Entry, APT-FORMS Application Development

3 The Oracle DBMS

This chapter is devoted to a general presentation of the Oracle DBMS. The functions outlined here, together with their implementation by Oracle, will be examined in more detail in subsequent chapters.

3.1 Background

The history of Oracle begins with the creation of Oracle Corporation in 1977. The first version, bascd on IBM's System-R specification, became a commercial product in 1979. It was one of the first commercial DBMSs. The period 1979 to 1984 saw the introduction of additional various tools designed to facilitate the use of Oracle. These included interfaces with high level languages like COBOL, C and FORTRAN, screen form management, report generators, and so on.

Oracle Corporation's response to the proliferation of microcomputers came in 1984 with the launch of the first PC version of Oracle. It was also one of the first truly relational DBMSs available on PCs. Other tools, such as the spreadsheet (SQL*Calc) have been developed around Oracle to assist its integration with the PC environment.

Another key factor in the history of Oracle's development was the launch of its first distributed version in 1986. Since then, further versions have followed to enhance the functions of distributed DBMSs.

In its current version Oracle is more than a relational DBMS. It is a working environment thanks to the wide range of tools based on SQL. These tools may be grouped into three categories:

- Application development tools. These allow the easy and fast development of applications around the database. There is a wide choice: screen form management, report generator, spreadsheet, etc.
- Distributed data management tools. These allow an Oracle application to access a database located on a remote site. They also allow access to data distributed over different sites.
- Tools for data administration. These allow the database administrator to supervise the database and ensure that it remains coherent. They

9

allow a database to be loaded from external files (from other software), data to be saved and restored, and so on.

3.2 Oracle: a relational DBMS

The Oracle DBMS has the standard functional qualities of a relational system. These are itemised below.

A – definition and manipulation of data
Oracle contains a language that allows data to be defined and manipulated. The manipulation is carried out in a non-procedural manner using the relational operators of SQL (projection, restriction, join, union, intersection and difference). SQL's commands may be used interactively or within an application program.

B – management of data coherence
Oracle ensures that each set of update operations on the database that constitutes a logical processing unit is executed completely or not at all ('all or nothing' principle). This logical processing unit is called a trans-action. Oracle allows transactions to be defined, verified or cancelled if there is a problem.

C – management of data confidentiality
Data confidentiality is assured under Oracle by means of the concept of privileges and views. Each user may have privileges for connection with the database via one of the Oracle tools, to create and manipulate different objects (tables, views, etc). He may be allocated a privilege to carry out an operation on an object that does not belong to him, and perhaps have the right to attribute this same privilege to other users. For example, a user may give others the right to change or remove his own objects. The database administrator is accorded a special privilege: the holder of this position can create users and carry out operations linked directly with data administration (save, drop, etc).

   In addition, views allow access to data to be restricted by only permitting access to a subset of the data in one or more tables.

D – management of integrity constraints
Integrity constraints may be fixed when the data is defined. Oracle ensures that these constraints are always verified at the moment of data update (insertion, modification, deletion). The integrity constraints are either defined implicitly by data types (number, character, date), or explicitly by keywords that state the optional or mandatory nature of data at the column level and the uniqueness of lines in a table.

E – security management
In order to restore the database to a coherent state following a hardware or software crash, Oracle has both warm and cold start techniques. These are based on the concept of journalisation using before and after images of the update operations.

F – management of concurrent access
Oracle's locking techniques allow several users to access the same data simultaneously. Locking is an integrity aspect that consists of barring access to part of the data while that data is being used by a processing unit. It thus enables data to be protected against update operations or those that affect the structure (made by several concurrent users). As a consequence of this technique, two users may find themselves in the position where each is waiting for a part of the data that the other is using. This is called deadlock. Oracle has methods of detecting such a situation which allow it to remove the lock from one user by following certain rules.

3.3 Oracle: an open architecture DBMS

In addition to the standard features of a DBMS, Oracle is distinguished by its open architecture. This is facilitated by

- its compatibility with other DBMSs
- the portability of the database and its applications
- the distribution of data and applications.

Compatibility with other DBMSs
As we shall see later, Oracle is built around an SQL layer that allows each command addressed to the database to be translated into SQL commands. The compatibility of Oracle's SQL version with that of other DBMSs, in particular SQL/DS and IBM's DB2, means that applications developed on other DBMSs can be used with a minimum of alteration. Applications developed under SQL/DS and DB2 can be executed under Oracle without major alteration. This is explained by the fact that Oracle is strongly inspired by System-R, which was developed by the originator of SQL/DS and DB2.

Portability of data and applications
Oracle is written in C and because of this is available on a wide variety of hardware and operating systems. So far as hardware is concerned, the range

extends from large machines (IBM 43xx, 30xx, Amdahl470, 580, etc) to microcomputers (IBM PC/XT, PC/AT, Macintosh and PS2). As for operating systems, the majority of existing systems support Oracle, the best known being Unix, VMS, MVS and DOS. All versions of Oracle on these different machines and operating systems are identical and offer the some facilities. As a result, porting an Oracle application from one machine to another may be carried out without major changes. This ensures a certain level of independence of Oracle data and applications *vis-à-vis* the hardware and software environment.

Distribution of data and applications
Oracle's availability on a wide variety of machines and the development of communication techniques allow both data and applications to be decentralised. This is possible through Oracle's open architecture. On the one hand, distributed access to data from applications located on different machines is possible; on the other hand, data can be distributed among different machines. This distribution can be made transparent to users.

4 Functional Architecture of Oracle

4.1 Basic architecture

The basic architecture of the Oracle DBMS is shown in figure 4.1. The facilities are organised in four layers. The kernel, the dictionary, and SQL make up the basic layers. The external layer consists of utilities and application development tools.

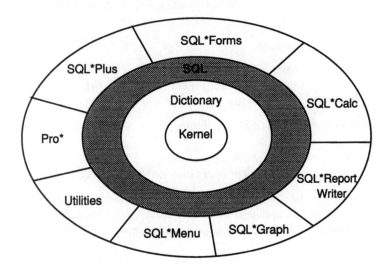

Figure 4.1 Basic architecture of Oracle

4.1.1 The kernel

The kernel is the first basic layer. It provides communication with the database and connection with other kernels in a distributed database environment. In addition to the facilities introduced in chapter 3 (verification of integrity constraints, verification of data coherence, control of concurrent access, data confidentiality management and restart from crash), the kernel ensures the following:

13

– Optimum request execution
The kernel includes an SQL integrated request optimiser. Any request sent to Oracle is optimised, then executed.

– Accelerator management
The kernel uses two types of accelerator to improve data access performance. The first is called an index, which is linked to a table and allows direct access to lines. The second accelerator type is the group, also called a cluster. It applies to tables that have common columns and/or those that are often accessed together.

– Physical data storage
The kernel uses the facilities of the host operating system (that is, the system on which Oracle is installed) to represent and store the database in the form of files. The contents of these files are managed by the kernel. Oracle thus preserves maximum independence from the operating system.

4.1.2 The data dictionary

The Oracle dictionary is a metabase which dynamically describes the database. At any time its contents reflect an image of the database. It can therefore describe the following in detail:

- the database objects (tables, columns, views, index, synonyms, clusters, etc)
- the system users (names and passwords)
- the privileges and rights of users over different objects.

Consequently, the contents of the dictionary constitute a set of data that evolves with use (as updated) of the database. Each operation that affects the structure of the database automatically causes the dictionary to be updated.

The main consequence of the description of all the objects controlled by Oracle in a data dictionary is the possibility of integrated manipulation of both the data and its structure (using SQL).

The dictionary can therefore be used for several purposes:

– Documentation
Any user who wishes may obtain information relating to the objects in the database. These may be objects that belong to him or objects which he has the right to manipulate. For this, according to the security rules defined in Oracle, each user has a restricted view of the dictionary that he may consult as a database. Such consultation may yield the names, definitions, meanings and properties of the data.

– Administration

Operations necessary for the administration of the database are included, in particular the control and management of user access authorisation. This requires database administration privilege.

The dictionary is made up of a set of tables and views that are manipulated through SQL. They are created, automatically, when Oracle is installed and they are updated when the database is manipulated. The tables in the dictionary are not directly accessible by users because the information that they contain is held in a 'coded' form and is therefore incomprehensible. Only a database administrator called SYS can manipulate these tables.

So far as views are concerned, these are derived from tables in the dictionary and may be consulted more easily, because they contain information that is more understandable to users.

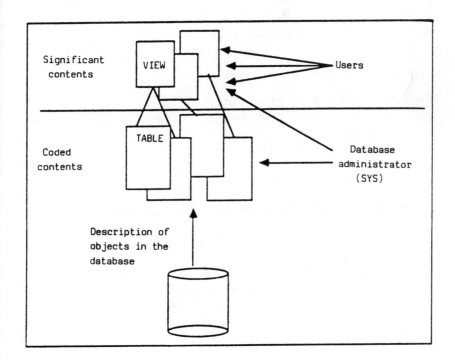

Figure 4.2 The data dictionary

The tables in the dictionary are created automatically when Oracle is installed. This is done with two special accounts SYS and SYSTEM both having the database administration privilege (DBA). The views of the dictionary belong to the SYSTEM account which has the additional right to select tables in the dictionary.

4.1.3 The SQL layer

This third and last basic layer acts as the interface between the kernel and the tools of the external layer. So, every access operation to the data is expressed in SQL.

SQL commands may be classified in two families. A first set of commands makes up the data definition language (DDL). It allows data structures to be created, modified and deleted (tables, views, index, etc).

The second family of commands, called the data manipulation language (DML), allows data in the database to be viewed, inserted, modified and deleted.

Use of the DDL and DML commands allows continuous development of the contents (data) and the structure (schema).

4.1.4 The external layer

This layer consists of a set of tools that enables all the facilities provided by the first three basic layers to be used easily. They offer an applications development environment.

SQL*Plus

This is a fourth generation interactive interface that allows the following:

- interactive use of SQL. Every SQL command can be initiated from SQL*Plus
- the work environment can be parameterised: line length, lines per page, automatic validation, etc
- formatting of results: the results from SQL requests can be formatted to produce reports on the screen or on paper (title, footer, total, etc)
- SQL and SQL*Plus commands can be stored in command files. A set of SQL and SQL*Plus commands can be grouped in the same command file and thus form a program or a procedure.

SQL*Forms

This is a tool that allows the database to be used by means of screen forms without the user having a previous knowledge of SQL. This provides the means of:

- developing applications based on screen forms without programming using menus

– selecting, modifying and deleting data without formulating SQL requests. Even quite complex SQL requests can be replaced by the use of a few function keys.

SQL*Report

This is a tool for producing reports. It only requires a limited number of commands to format the results of a request. Elaborate reports can then be produced incorporating features such as page numbering, headers and footers, titles, calculations of totals and subtotals, and so on.

It also allows text to be mixed with the results of SQL requests, a very useful facility for applications such as mailings.

SQL*Graph

This is a decision-making tool that allows the results of SQL requests to be presented in graphical form. A range of different graphical shapes is available, including curves, point clusters, histograms and pie charts.

SQL*Calc

This tool combines the power of a spreadsheet with that of SQL. It is in fact a Lotus 1-2-3 compatible spreadsheet that offers the additional facility to assign SQL commands to the spreadsheet cells.

On the one hand it can automatically load data from the database into the spreadsheet and, on the other hand, it can update the database from operations carried out on the spreadsheet. The contents of a cell can be an SQL request. It is also possible to create Oracle tables from the spreadsheet.

SQL*Menu

This tool allows one to define and choose between several actions presented in the form of one or more menus. The actions generally correspond to the execution of commands from Oracle tools such as SQL*Plus, SQL*Forms or SQL*Report, or commands from the host system. The execution of different actions in an application can be arranged using the menus.

Programmable interfaces

Oracle contains a variety of programming interfaces that allow access from high level languages like C, COBOL, FORTRAN, PL/1, Pascal and Ada to data controlled by the Oracle system. These interfaces are precompilers that translate SQL commands inserted in a program written in the host language. Precompilers currently available include PRO*COBOL, PRO*C, PRO*-FORTRAN, PRO*PL/1, PRO*PASCAL and PRO*ADA.

4.2 Distributed architecture of Oracle

In a network environment, Oracle uses a model called client-server (to distinguish it from the data models presented in chapter 2). A client may be any application requiring data from an Oracle database. A server is a machine controlling an Oracle database.

Relying on this model, Oracle allows applications and data to be distributed. Furthermore, it is not restricted to its own data, but is open to the data from other systems, particularly from SQL/DS and DB2.

4.2.1 Distributed applications

Oracle offers the facility of accessing a database from applications supported by machines (clients) that are remote from the one that controls the database (server). This allows some machines to be dedicated to applications while others are managing the data. The server is thus relieved of the task of handling applications.

SQL*Net is an Oracle tool that allows the connection of one application executing on one client machine to an Oracle kernel executing on a server machine. The client sends its formatted request to the server in the form of messages. These messages are received by the server which decodes them into SQL requests, executes them through the Oracle kernel and returns the results to the client.

So that SQL*Net can be used in different networks, there is a set of communication protocols. Each protocol contains a driver.

4.2.2 Distributed data

Data controlled by Oracle may be localised on different sites. When a database is set up, fragments of data can be stored at different sites. The set of localised data at different sites constitutes a distributed database.

Oracle also allows cooperation beteen existing databases. Localised data at different sites that model the same universe, or universes that have certain links, can be used at the same time. SQL*Star makes this possible; it is made up of three elements:

– SQL*Net
– a distributed kernel
– SQL*Connect.

In addition to the standard local data management functions, the distributed kernel ensures execution of multi-database requests. To exchange data with other Oracle kernels, it uses the facilities of SQL*Net. To access non-Oracle data, it calls upon SQL*Connect. The latter allows the use of Oracle tools and Oracle SQL facilities that are not available in other DBMSs.

4.2.3 Opening to other DBMSs

In its distributed architecture, Oracle is not restricted to the data controlled by the kernels located at different sites. It allows cooperation with other DBMSs. This means that data controlled by DB2 or SQL/DS can be accessed from Oracle applications.

A set of tools is available to include other DBMSs.

5 Introduction to SQL

5.1 Background

The Structured Query Language (SQL) is a standard established for the definition and manipulation of relational databases. It consists of a set of commands that allow the definition, manipulation and control of data in a relational database.

The history of SQL begins with D. Chamberlain and R. Boyce's proposal in 1974 of a language called SEQUEL, followed in turn by SQUARE and then SEQUEL 2. The latter was used as a query language in IBM's System R. The current name of SQL dates from 1980.

Work on the standardisation of SQL began in 1982. The ANSI committee called X3H2 had been charged with the task of proposing a relational language. The first standard was published in 1986; it was based essentially on IBM's version of SQL.

Today, there are many implementations of SQL, but there are only a few that are totally compatible with the ANSI standard, including SQL/DS and DB2.

In all that follows, we shall consider Oracle's implementation of that standard. So, each time that we mention SQL, this should be interpreted as Oracle's SQL. In this chapter we will give an example of a database that will be used in the subsequent chapters. In the next three chapters we present in turn the data definition, manipulation and control commands. Views are a special case because they introduce at the same time both the definition and manipulation of data. They will therefore be treated along with data control.

5.2 A database example

In the following chapters, we will illustrate the use of the Oracle DBMS by a conventional example of the operations of a company that produces and sells furniture.

We assume that the company is centrally organised, so far as manufacture, warehousing and marketing are concerned. The company has a fixed number of sales agents grouped under the same agency. Initially, the management rules are quite simple. However, we shall have occasion to make new hypotheses to illustrate unforeseen procedures. The company has a stock of products that it markets. The amount of stock of each item is known. Access to the database for an enquiry concerning the stock level enables a salesman to know immediately whether or not he can fulfil the orders from clients with whom he deals.

The initial information system that models this company consists of the following entities. Each entity is described by its characteristics.

CLIENT
- clientid : client number
- name : client name
- address : client address
- postcode : postcode
- town : postal town
- tel : telephone
- specterms : special terms (discounts, bad payer comment, etc)

PRODUCT
- productid : product identifier
- designation : product designation
- unitprice : unit price
- qtystock : quantity in stock

ORDER
- ordernum : order number
- orderdate : order date
- productid : product identifier
- qtyord : order quantity
- clientid : client number

SALE
- ordernum : order number
- agentnum : sales agent number
- paydate : date of payment

The sales agency that we shall examine consists of two salesmen (sa1, sa2), each of whom has a terminal from which he can access the database.

5.3 Basic objects

We shall now introduce the basic objects that Oracle manipulates. These are:

– tables
– views
– users and their privileges on tables and/or views
– accelerators (indexes, clusters) on tables.

The reader may be surprised to see no mention of the concept of a database in these objects. In Oracle a user may not explicitly define a database. But in an implicit way, the set of tables and views created by a user makes up what is for him his default database. This set of tables and views constitutes his universe when he makes a connection using one of the Oracle tools. However, he may access other tables and views created by other users by prefixing them with the name of that user and provided that he has the necessary privileges.

In figure 5.1 user1 has created two tables Table1 and Table2 and view View1. The two tables are grouped in the same cluster because they are often accessed together. This same user can access table Table3 via view View2. User3 has created an indexed table Table3 and two views View2 and View3 on this table. Finally, user2 has created no table or view, but has the privilege of accessing table Table2 by prefixing it with the name of user1.

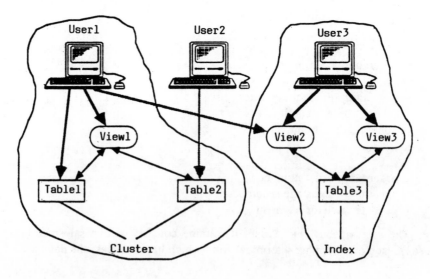

Figure 5.1 Objects manipulated by Oracle

Tables

In a relational type DBMS, the information is seen in the form of tables. A table is identified by a name and corresponds to a set of values (table of values) in two dimensions. It describes an entity or an association between two entities. The name of a table must be unique for a given user. To designate a table belonging to (that is, created by) another user, its name must be prefixed with that user's name. A table is constructed horizontally from a set of columns, each corresponding to a characteristic (or an attribute) of the entity. The set of values taken by a column is defined by its type. If a value is undefined, it is said to be a null value (that is, non-zero and belonging to the empty set).

A line in the table is formed by a value from each column and represents an occurrence of the entity.

A column is described by a name and a data type. The name is unique for the same table, but it can designate two columns in two different tables. The designation of the column is made by prefixing it with the name of the table if there is any ambiguity. We say that the column is qualified by the name of the table. There is an assumed order (from left to right) between the columns in a table. The number of columns determines the degree of the table.

It should be noted that there is no concept of order between lines. However, one can specify an order of presentation when making a selection. The number of lines is called the cardinality of the table.

Example 5.1

The information that describes clients in the example is organised in a table called Client. Each column represents a characteristic of the client entity. So the first column in figure 5.2, clientid, represents the client number. The second column represents his name, and the remaining columns, called respectively address, postcode, town, tel and specterm, represent the client's address, postcode, town, telephone number and special terms.

Views

A view is a virtual table; that is, a table that does not exist physically. It is an object whose definition derives from those of tables and/or views. A view may be thought of as the satisfaction of a database query (difference operators from relational algebra). In fact, the definition of the view is stored (in the dictionary) in the form of a query. On execution, the definition of the view is substituted for the view reference and then executed as part of the command.

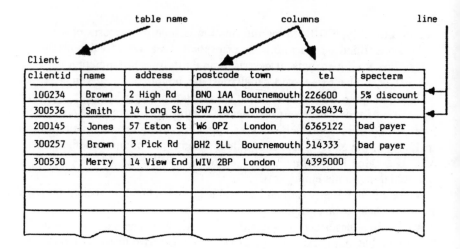

clientid	name	address	postcode	town	tel	specterm
100234	Brown	2 High Rd	BNO 1AA	Bournemouth	226600	5% discount
300536	Smith	14 Long St	SW7 1AX	London	7368434	
200145	Jones	57 Eston St	W6 0PZ	London	6365122	bad payer
300257	Brown	3 Pick Rd	BH2 5LL	Bournemouth	514333	bad payer
300530	Merry	14 View End	WIV 2BP	London	4395000	

Figure 5.2 Example of the contents of the Client table. (Note that the details in this table are purely fictitious. Any resemblance to a real person is completely coincidental.)

Example 5.2

Figure 5.3 shows the view of bad payers, termed Badpayers, derived from the table Client; it has the same structure as Client but only contains those clients whose particular conditions are that they are bad payers. This is known as a restriction.

Result of
selection
from view
of all
bad payers

Client

clientid	name	address	postcode	town	tel	specterm
100234	Brown	2 High Rd	BNO 1AA	Bournemouth	226600	5% discount
300536	Smith	14 Long St	SW7 1AX	London	7368434	
200145	Jones	57 Eston St	W6 0PZ	London	6365122	bad payer
300257	Brown	3 Pick Rd	BH2 5LL	Bournemouth	514333	bad payer
300530	Merry	14 View End	WIV 2BP	London	4395000	

Figure 5.3 Example of the contents of the view Badpayers

Users

A user in Oracle is defined by a name (unique identifier), a password and a set of privileges (or rights). The concept of privilege allows the rules governing the use of objects defined in the database to be established and, as a result, ensures the confidentiality of data.

To carry out any operation on an object, a user must have the necessary privileges. These are associated with the following operations: SELECT, INSERT, UPDATE and DELETE. The owner of a table possesses all these privileges on that table.

Accelerators

Oracle has two mechanisms for improving performance at the access level of databases: indexes and clusters (or groups). Indexes are tables that contain for each line the physical address of the page where the values of this line are stored. Clusters are physical groups of data. These store data that is often accessed together in the same page(s) of backing store.

6 Data Definition in SQL

6.1 Introduction

The definition of data in SQL allows objects manipulated by the DBMS to be described. These objects can be logical objects or physical objects. Logical objects are grouped into tables and synonyms. The physical objects are the physical representation of the data – spaces, indexes and groups. The definition of physical objects is discussed in chapter 14 on data administration.

SQL's data definition commands, also called verbs, are:

- CREATE : to create objects
- ALTER : to alter the structure of objects
- DROP : to delete objects.

6.2 Defining tables

The operations for defining tables cover creation, alteration of the structure and deletion. Renaming remains an operation restricted to Oracle itself.

6.2.1 Creating tables

Creating a table consists of defining its name, the columns that it contains and their types. The command CREATE TABLE is used. Oracle has two forms for this command which are described below.

First form. This is the simpler and most frequently used. It allows an empty table to be created. The syntax is as follows:

```
CREATE TABLE table (column definition,...);
```

The table designation is a unique name, for any given user, that allows identification of the table in the database. In addition, it must not be the same as any SQL keyword.

Defining a column consists of specifying in turn its name, its type and its size. Integrity constraints may be defined by stating whether NULL values in the column are allowed.

```
name_of_column type [(size)] [NULL | NOT NULL]
```

The type defines the column type. In contrast to the SQL standard where the type defines the internal data representation (integer, decimal, floating point, etc), Oracle SQL allows the type to be defined according to the external appearance of the data (number, character string or date). However, the first definition style is still possible in Oracle. The size indicates the maximum size that a column may attain. If the NOT NULL option is included, the column may not contain the null value. This option is mainly used for columns that serve as a key in a table.

The data types possible in Oracle are

- CHAR (n) and VARCHAR (n) : a string of n characters; n must not exceed 240
- DATE : date, for which the standard form is DD-MM-YY
- LONG, LONG VARCHAR : character string of variable size up to 65,535 characters. A single column per table can be of type LONG. Columns of this type may not be used in sub-queries, functions, expressions, WHERE clauses and in indexes. Similarly, a cluster may be defined in a table that has a LONG type column
- NUMBER : integer or decimal up to maximum of 40 places.
  Numbers may be specified in two ways:
  – the digits 0 to 9, + and – signs, and the decimal point
  – using scientific notation (for example, 1.85E3 for 1850)
- NUMBER (n) : the same as NUMBER with a specified size. The maximum value for n is 105
- NUMBER (n,m) : a decimal number having a maximum number of n digits with m digits after the decimal point
- DECIMAL, INTEGER and SMALLINT : same as NUMBER
- RAW (n) : a binary number of n bytes, with n not exceeding 240. This type defines a pseudo column (internal) that identifies a line in a table. The columns in a table may not be of this type
- LONGRAW : like RAW.

Example 6.1
The following command creates a table for the client entity in our basic example. We shall assume that the client number (clientid) is the entity identifier. For this reason, it is defined with the NOT NULL option. It should be noted that this single condition is insufficient to guarantee the uniquenes of clients (see creating an index).

```
CREATE TABLE Client
    (clientid NUMBER(6) NOT NULL,
```

```
name CHAR(20),
address CHAR(80),
postcode CHAR(6),
town CHAR(10),
tel NUMBER(10),
specterm CHAR(50));
```

Second form. Apart from defining the structure of a new table, the second form of the command **CREATE TABLE** allows data to be inserted from one or more tables and/or views. In this context we speak of source tables and target tables. The target table is the one to be created and the source table(s) is the one from which the data is copied. The command syntax is as follows:

```
CREATE TABLE table [(column [NOT NULL],...)]
     AS query;
```

The query is a selection operation that indicates the source columns, the tables to which they belong and perhaps some selection criteria.

The specification of columns is not obligatory in this second form. If it is done, it is confined to naming the columns and possibly prescribing null values. The type and size of the columns will be inherited from the columns given in the query in the order in which they appear. The number of columns mentioned must match the number of columns selected in the query.

If no column name is given, the newly created table will have as its column names those indicated in the selection query, still in the order of their appearance.

Example 6.2

Suppose we wish to create a table containing only the London clients. We shall no longer need the postcode and town. The create command for this new table, which we call Client_london, is as follows:

```
CREATE TABLE Client_london
    AS   SELECT clientid, name, tel,
         specterm
         FROM Client
         WHERE town = 'London';
```

The result of this command is a table containing as columns: clientid, name, tel and specterm. The table will include all the lines relating to the clients whose town is London.

When a table is created, Oracle defines the data storage space that needs to be allocated. This definition allows the minimum and maximum space used by the table to be fixed in relation to the total size of the database. The definition of these parameters is optional in the two forms of the CREATE TABLE command and it is done with the following clause which appears immediately after the column definition. The syntax is:

```
SPACE define_space [PCTFREE n]
```

where define_space is a pre-assigned identifier created by a space defining command CREATE SPACE [DEFINITION]. The PCTFREE option specifies the percentage of space to keep free for updates and has the same meaning as the command CREATE SPACE [DEFINITION]. Here it redefines the value already established by this command.

It is also possible to include the table to be created in an existing cluster in order to improve performance (see the command CREATE CLUSTER). If it exists, this option must follow the definition of the columns and the definition of space if there is one. The syntax of the appropriate clause is:

```
CLUSTER group (column,...)
```

where group designates a predefined group created by the command CREATE CLUSTER, and column designates the columns in the group.

6.2.2 Altering table structures

The tables controlled by Oracle may have a dynamic structure. This dynamism is expressed by the ability to be able to add new columns and/or alter already existing column types. Deleting columns is not directly possible. One method of doing this is to create, from the initial table, a new table excluding the deleted columns. The second form of the command CREATE TABLE is used with a slightly different table name. The two possibilities for altering tables are carried out by the two variants of the command ALTER TABLE.

First form. The first variant of the command allows new columns to be added to a table. The syntax is:

```
ALTER TABLE table ADD (column_definition,...);
```

where column_definition is the same form as that used in the command CREATE TABLE. The columns are added on the right of the last column in the table and they all have null values. In the definition of the columns to be added, it is therefore only possible to specify the option NOT NULL if the table has as yet no line.

Example 6.3

We will add a client_type column to the Client_london table to enable clients to be classified. We will assume that three characters are sufficient for this purpose.

```
ALTER TABLE Client_london ADD (client_type CHAR(3));
```

Second form. The second variant allows alteration of existing column types. The possible alterations are:

- increase the size: always possible
- reduce the size: only if the column contains null values
- alter the type: as for reducing size
- deleting the ban on including null values (NOT NULL instead of NULL): always possible.

The appropriate command has the following syntax:

```
ALTER TABLE table MODIFY (column_definition,...);
```

Here too, column_definition has the same syntax and meaning as the command **CREATE TABLE.**

Example 6.4
Suppose that three characters are now insufficient to code client types and we need to add a further two. Changing to five characters is achieved as follows:

```
ALTER TABLE Client_london MODIFY (client_type CHAR(5));
```

6.2.3 Deleting tables

The dynamic nature of an Oracle database is not restricted to adding other tables or columns at any time or altering those in existence. It applies equally in the opposite direction. Some tables may in certain cases cease to be useful. This is the case with working tables created for intermediate use which then need to be deleted.

In Oracle the command to delete is:

```
DROP TABLE table;
```

Deleting a table means deleting the associated synonyms and indexes. The views created on the table become obsolete; they must be redefined, taking account of the deletion made.

6.2.4 Renaming and creating table synonyms

Oracle offers the possibility of changing the name of a table after it has been created. This is done with the command:

```
RENAME old_name TO new_name;
```

where new_name is substituted for old_name.

This command must be used with care, especially when there are views or applications based on the table. In this case, appropriate alterations must also be made to the definition of the applications and views. The concept of the synonym makes this problem somewhat easier. It involves attributing one or more additional names, called synonyms (SYNONYM), to a table, while still retaining the original name. The table can then be designated by its original name or by the synonym. Thus, views and applications that have been defined using the original name require no alteration. The syntax of this command is:

```
CREATE SYNONYM synonym_name FOR table;
```

where synonym_name is the synonym to be attributed and table is the original name of the table.

Deleting a synonym is effected with the command:

```
DROP SYNONYM synonym;
```

Another use of this command is to abbreviate table names, especially when they are too long. A user may, in certain cases, and if properly authorised, manipulate tables belonging to other users. In this case, he is obliged to prefix each table name with the owner's user name. This can become tedious in practice. Using synonyms removes this burden.

When the user wishes to emphasise certain table names, he can make use of synonyms.

Example 6.5

Suppose that the table Client belongs to a user identified by Bloggs and there is another user who may have to manipulate this table quite often. He will then have to designate it each time with 'Bloggs.Client'. By creating a synonym 'Client_B' using the following command:

```
CREATE SYNONYM Client_B FOR Bloggs.Client;
```

he can then use either of these names.

The ability to use synonyms helps to support a local aspect peculiar to a user.

7 Data Manipulation in SQL

7.1 Displaying data

7.1.1 Simple table search

The simplest form of a query consists of searching all the lines of a given table. The syntax is:

```
SELECT *
FROM table;
```

where table is the table or view name to be consulted. The * character indicates that all the columns of a table are required. A query formulated in this way is equivalent to: 'list all the contents of a table'.

Example 7.1
List the contents of the Client table:

```
SELECT *
FROM Client;
```

In practice, it is rare to require all the columns in a table. More usually only a few are required. In this case, the SELECT clause takes the following form:

```
SELECT column,...
FROM table
```

Example 7.2
List the name and town of all clients:

```
SELECT name, town
FROM Client;
```

The result of a query is displayed in tabular form. The heading is made up of the column names in the order of their appearance in the SELECT clause, or in the order in which they were given when the table was created if the * character is mentioned in SELECT. However, it is possible to

32

choose different heading names for columns by specifying them in the SELECT clause. Such headings are called aliases. The syntax for the SELECT clause then becomes:

```
SELECT column [alias],...
```

If alias consists of more than one word, it must be included within quote marks.

Example 7.3
To select the identifier and name of each client.

```
SELECT clientid "Client number", name
FROM Client;
```

In the result, the clientid column will be designated by "Client number".

7.1.2 Search with qualification

In the majority of cases, search queries are not concerned with a table in its totality. Only a few lines therefore need to be selected depending on certain conditions. Such conditions may be expressed by the WHERE clause which comes after the FROM clause and has the following syntax:

```
WHERE condition
```

The condition is generally made up of three terms:

• a column name
• a comparison operator
• a constant, a column name, or a list of values.

The following common comparison operators are available:

```
=           : equal
!= or <>  : different
<           : less than
<=          : less than or equal
>           : greater than
>=          : greater than or equal.
```

In addition, Oracle contains other specific operators:

IS NULL : tests whether the content of a column is a null value.

IN (list of values) : tests whether the content of a column coincides with one of the values in the list.

BETWEEN v1 AND v2 : tests if the content of a column lies between the two values v1 and v2 (>= v1 and <= v2).

LIKE generic string : tests if the content of a column resembles a character string obtained from the generic string. The latter is a string of characters in which there is one of the following generic characters:

% any character string, including the empty string
_ any character.

The string to be compared is therefore obtained by substituting the generic character with a character or a string in the generic string. For example, the generic string 'Sm%' is equivalent to any string beginning with 'Sm' such as 'Smith', 'Smart', 'Smythe', etc, whereas the generic string 'SMIT_' is equivalent to a five-character string whose fifth character is any character. The strings SMITH and SMITE are examples of valid strings.

All the specific operators may be put in negative form by prefixing them with the negation operator NOT. We therefore have IS NOT NULL, NOT IN, NOT BETWEEN and NOT LIKE.

Example 7.4
1) Select all products with less than ten units in stock

```
SELECT *
FROM Product
WHERE qtystock < 10;
```

2) Select the designation and unit price of products whose unit price lies between £50 and £100.

```
SELECT designation, unitprice
FROM  Product
WHERE unitprice BETWEEN 50 AND 100;
```

3) Select clients in London, Bournemouth and Manchester

```
SELECT *
FROM Client
WHERE town IN ('London', 'Bournemouth', 'Manchester');
```

The condition in the WHERE clause may be a composite condition, that is, two or more conditions linked by the logical operators AND and OR.

Example 7.5
Select the designation and unit price of products available whose unit price lies between £50 and £100.

```
SELECT designation, unitprice
FROM Product
WHERE unitprice BETWEEN 50 AND 100
AND qtystock > 0;
```

7.1.3 Arithmetic expressions

Arithmetic expressions may be used in SELECT or WHERE clauses. The formulation of these expressions uses:

- column names
- constants
- the arithmetic operators: +, -, * and /
- arithmetic functions.

The arithmetic functions available in SQL Oracle are:

```
ABS (n)      absolute value of n
CEIL (n)     the smallest integer greater than or equal to n
FLOOR (n)    the integer part of n
MOD (m,n)    the remainder of the integer division of m by n
POWER (m,n)  m raised to the power of n
ROUND (n,m)  n rounded to a number with m decimal places. m may be
omitted if it is equal to 0.
SIGN (n)     -1 if n < 0
              0 if n = 0
              1 if n > 0
SQRT (n)     the square root of n
TRUNC (n,m)  n truncated to m decimal places after the point. If m
is negative, truncation is made before the decimal point.
```

The arithmetic expressions only apply to numeric type columns.

Example 7.6
1) Give the price in French francs given an exchange rate of £1 = 9.38F.

```
SELECT designation, unitprice*9.38 ''price in francs''
FROM Product;
```

2) Give the prices of all products rounded in pounds.

```
SELECT designation, ROUND(unitprice) ''price in pounds''
FROM Product;
```

7.1.4 Aggregate functions

The arithmetic functions apply to a single value in a column. They are single variable functions. Oracle contains another family of functions called aggregate functions that apply to a set of values in a column. These functions allow information to be obtained that relates to a set of data, such as the average, maximum or minimum value, or the sum of a series of values. These functions are:

```
AVG         : arithmetic mean
COUNT       : number of occurrences
MAX         : maximum value
MIN         : minimum value
STDDEV      : standard deviation
SUM         : sum
VARIANCE    : variance.
```

Each of these functions has as its argument a column name or an arithmetic expression (whose result is a numeric value). They take no account of null values. The column or expression to which an aggregate function is applied may have values that repeat. To indicate that all values or only distinctive values are to be included, the column or expression needs to be prefixed with DISTINCT or ALL. If no indication is given, ALL is the default.

The function COUNT may take as argument the * character. In this case, it returns as result the number of selected lines.

Example 7.7
1) Find the number of clients in the town of London.

```
SELECT COUNT(*)
FROM Client
WHERE town = 'London';
```

2) Find the average of the product unit prices.

```
SELECT AVG(unitprice)
FROM Product;
```

Notes
(i) It is not possible to have in the same SELECT clause a query to select an aggregate function and a column name or an expression. The following formulation is invalid:

```
SELECT designation, AVG(unitprice)...
```

The reason for this is that the designation column will have as many values as selected lines, whereas the AVG function returns a unique value, namely the average price of all the selected products.
(ii) Aggregate functions may not be used in the WHERE clause, in contrast to arithmetic functions which may be used in SELECT and WHERE clauses. This is explained by the fact that arithmetic functions apply individually to lines in the same way as the WHERE clause condition, whereas aggregate functions apply to a group of lines.

7.1.5 Other functions

Oracle has functions that apply to all types of data (numeric, character strings and dates). We have already seen the arithmetic functions that apply to numeric data. We shall now briefly review the main functions for manipulating character strings and the date. Full details will be found in the Oracle manuals.

Functions for manipulating character strings
The main functions are:

INITCAP (ch) : makes the first letter of each word in the string a capital
INSTAR (ch1, ch2, n, m) : locates the mth occurrence of ch2 in ch1 from character n. If n and m are omitted, they have a default value of 1
LENGTH (ch) : length of ch
LOWER (ch) : change ch to lower case
SUBSTR (ch, m, n) : withdraw a substring of ch starting at the mth character and of length n. If n is omitted, take the remainder of the string
TRANSLATE (ch, origin, target) : wherever the characters given in origin occur in ch, transforms them into the characters given in target
UPPER (ch) : change ch to upper case
ch1 I ch2 : concatenate ch1 and ch2.

Date manipulation functions
The main functions for manipulating dates are:

ADD_MONTHS (d,n) : add n months to date d
GREATEST (d1, d2) : the more recent date of d1 and d2
LEAST (d1, d2) : the older date of d1 and d2
MONTHS_BETWEEN (d1, d2) : number of months between d1 and d2.

Conversion functions
The conversion functions allow transformations of data types to be made. The main functions are:

TO_CHAR (d or n, format) : converts a date d or numeric value n into a character string as specified by format
TO_DATE (ch, format) : converts a character string representing a date ch into a date value as specified in format
TO_NUMBER (ch) : converts a character string representing a number ch into a number.

7.1.6 Nested queries

In a selective search operation, the values used in the selection condition may form part of the database. A typical example is one that involves selecting all the products whose unit price is greater than the unit price of a particular product termed x located in the database.

There are three possible ways of carrying out this type of operation:
– Divide the selection operation into two stages:
i) find the price of product x
ii) find all the other products whose price is greater than that of x

The disadvantage of this approach is the need for the user to manipulate an intermediate result.
– Make a theta-join; this possibility will be examined later in the chapter.
– The third way of solving the problem uses nested queries.

A query nested within another query is called a sub-query. It is formulated in the same way as any other search query except that it must be enclosed in parentheses. A sub-query may itself have another sub-query within it, and so on. The number of nested queries depends on the Oracle configuration. We will now describe the different cases where sub-queries might be used.
a) The result of a sub-query is formed from a single value: this is particularly true of sub-queries using an aggregate function in the SELECT clause.

Example 7.8
1) Find the products whose unit price is greater than the average unit price.

```
SELECT *
FROM Product
WHERE unitprice > (SELECT AVG(unitprice)
                            FROM Product);
```

2) Find the designation of all products whose unit price is equal to the product designated by 'chair'.

```
SELECT designation
FROM Product
WHERE unitprice = (SELECT unitprice
                  FROM Product
                  WHERE designation = 'chair');
```

b) The result of the sub-query is made up of a set of values: in this case, the result of the comparison, in the WHERE clause, may be considered to be true:
– either if the condition is satisfied with at least one of the values resulting from the sub-query

– or if the condition is satisfied for all values.

In the first case, the sub-query is prefixed with ANY and in the second with ALL.

```
The form of the query is as follows:
SELECT column,...
FROM table
WHERE column = ANY | ALL (sub-query);
```

An alternative form for "= ANY" is IN.

c) The result of the sub-query is a set of columns: if a sub-query returns more than one column, these may be compared simultaneously with the same number of columns in the WHERE clause of the global query. These columns must be placed within parentheses. The form of such a query is:

```
SELECT column,...
   FROM table
   WHERE (columns,...) = (sub-query);
```

The number of columns in the WHERE clause of the global query must correspond to the number of columns in the SELECT clause of the sub-query. The comparison is made between the values in the global query column and those in the sub-query column pair by pair. Suppose that the sub-query returns the list (scol1, scol2,...); the comparison is then equivalent to the expression (col1 = scol1) AND (col2 = scol2) AND...

d) The result of the sub-query is a logical value: it may be sufficient to know if the result of a sub-query contains or does not contain data (is an empty set or not). In this case, the values themselves are of no interest. The condition of the WHERE clause is true if the result is not empty and is false in the contrary case. A query of this form appears as follows:

```
SELECT column,...
   FROM table
   WHERE EXISTS (sub-query);
```

7.1.7 Sorting results

It is possible in Oracle to place results in an order. The order may be increasing or decreasing on one or more columns or expressions. This sequencing is obtained by adding to the query a clause called ORDER BY which takes the following form:

```
ORDER BY expression [ASC | DESC],...
```

where expression is based on one or more columns mentioned in the SELECT clause. The options ASC (ascending) and DESC (descending) indicate the direction in which the results are to be ordered. Ascending order is the default. If several expressions are indicated, the order is made according to the first expression. If there are lines with the same value for this expression, then the order follows the second expression, and so on.

When no ORDER BY clause is given, the order of the results is random (depending on storage, see management of physical space in chapter 14 on data administration).

Example 7.9
Give a list of products in sequence of increasing unit price, and for those that have the same price in alphabetical order.

```
SELECT designation, unitprice, qtystock
   FROM Product
   ORDER BY unitprice, designation;
```

7.1.8 Classification of results

Apart from sorting the results of a query, it is possible to group or classify the results. The classification enables one to group together the result lines in classes of equal value for a given column, to carry out a calculation such as finding the average or the sum of the values in the group and then display the result in the form of a line per group. The GROUP BY clause is used. It must follow the WHERE clause (or FROM if WHERE is not present) and has the syntax:

```
GROUP BY column,...
```

The columns must be given in SELECT. It is possible to make a multi-column group by mentioning several columns in the GROUP BY clause. This allows one to have sub-groups within a group. In the final display we obtain a line for each most atomic sub-group, that is, a group that has no sub-group. If there is a GROUP BY clause, the aggregate functions apply to the set of values of each group or sub-group.

Example 7.10
1) Find the sum of the quantities ordered per product in product sequence.

```
SELECT productid, SUM(qtyord)
   FROM Order
   GROUP BY productid;
```

In the response to this query we have a line for each product.
2) Suppose now that a client may make several orders for the same product and we want to find the sum of the quantities ordered by product and by client.

```
SELECT productid, clientid, SUM(qtyord)
FROM Order
GROUP BY productid, clientid;
```

Here we obtain as many result lines for each product as there are individual clients who have ordered this product. Each line contains the product number, the client number and the sum of the quantities ordered by that client.

We can make a selection in the GROUP BY clause. Such a selection can ensure that some groups that do not fulfil a given condition are eliminated; this is done with the HAVING clause in the following syntax:

```
HAVING condition;
```

The condition allows a value of the group to be compared with a constant or another value resulting from a sub-query.

It is important to distinguish clearly between the condition of the WHERE clause which applies to all lines and that of the HAVING clause which applies to a group or sub-group.

Example 7.11
Find the sum of the quantities ordered by product and by client. Ignore products whose cumulative orders by client are less than 10.

```
SELECT productid, clientid, SUM(qtyord)
    FROM Order
    GROUP BY productid, clientid
    HAVING SUM(qtyord) > = 10;
```

7.1.9 Join and cartesian product

In all the operations that we have described, we have only considered a single table. The data to be searched may be stored in different tables and/ or views. Furthermore, to obtain a result, it might be necessary to bring together data located in different tables. The operations that allow such data to be brought together are the cartesian product and the join.

Cartesian product
The cartesian product consists of swapping all the data in one table with another. This operation is carried out by specifying the tables to be swapped in the FROM clause and the result columns in the SELECT clause.

Note that great care is needed in using this operation because it imposes penalties both in response time and in the memory space required for its execution.

Join

Joining two tables allows the contents to be brought together to facilitate a comparison of the values in their common columns. The columns used for the comparison are called join columns. The result of a join is a third table whose columns derive from the two tables and the lines are those from the two tables that satisfy the comparison criterion.

A join is in fact nothing more than a cartesian product followed by a selection (or restriction) using the WHERE clause. Its formulation is therefore quite close to that of the cartesian product. It requires first that the tables to be brought together be indicated in the FROM clause in the same way as for a cartesian product; then follows the joining criterion in the form of a condition in the WHERE clause.

The general form of a join query is:

```
SELECT column,...
   FROM table [variable], table [variable],...
   WHERE condition;
```

The names of the columns in the SELECT and WHERE clause must be unique. If two columns of the two tables have the same name and must appear in the results or the condition, they should be prefixed by the name of the tables. There is the likelihood that the resulting name will be quite long and might be the source of error in the formulation of the query. This can be prevented by using variables for table names. Then in the FROM clause a variable can be attributed to each table that might be referred to in other parts of the query.

We have mentioned above that there are various types of join. The type is determined by the condition in the WHERE clause. The simplest and most often used form is called an equi-join, where the comparison operator involved is equality.

Example 7.12

1) Find the client name for order number 1234.

```
SELECT name
FROM Client cl, Order or
WHERE cl.clientid = or.clientid
AND ordernum = 1234;
```

2) Give a list of orders with, in addition to the columns of the Order table, the client name.

```
SELECT or.*, cl.name
FROM Client cl, Order or
WHERE cl.clientid = or.clientid;
```

Note in this example the use of the * character. It designates all columns of the table linked with the variable or (the order table).

When the comparison operator is not equality (that is, <, <=, >, >=), the corresponding operation is called a theta-join.

Example 7.13
Find the designation and the unit price of products whose price is greater than that of product x.

```
SELECT p1.designation, p1.unitprice
FROM Product p1, Product p2
WHERE p1.unitprice > p2.unitprice
AND p2.designation = 'x';
```

This example illustrates the special case of joining a table with itself; that is, auto-joining. The use of variables cannot be avoided here.

External join
In addition to the conventional joining operations (known as internal joins), Oracle also allows external joins (outer-join).

In conventional equi-joins, the lines in the first table that have no corresponding line in the second table do not form part of the result. Outer joining allows these lines to be preserved by placing null values in the columns of the result corresponding to the second table.

From the syntax point of view, this operation is formulated in the same way as the other joins, except that it is necessary to follow the join criterion with the plus sign within parentheses (+) in the WHERE clause.

Example 7.14
Give the list of products with any orders that relate to them.

```
SELECT p.*, o.ordernum
    FROM Product p, Order o
    WHERE p.productid = o.productid (+);
```

Those products that have no order will still be part of the display, which is not true of an internal join.

7.1.10 Union

The union operation consists of making the union between the results of two queries, provided that these results are compatible, that is, they have the same munber of columns and the same types of data for columns in the same position.

The form of a union operation is:

```
query1
  UNION
  query2
```

7.1.11 Intersection

Intersection returns lines that are common to the results of two queries. The results must also be compatible so far as their structures are concerned. The form of this operation is:

```
query1
  INTERSECT
  query2
```

7.1.12 Difference

The MINUS operator returns lines that appear in the result of the first query and not in the result of the second.

```
query1
  MINUS
  query2
```

7.2 Modifying data

The operation for modifying data consists of updating the columns in a table with new values. Each new value may be given explicitly in the modification command or be obtained from the database by a sub-query. The normal form of this command is;

```
UPDATE table
  SET column = value,...
  WHERE condition;
```

It is not possible to update more than one table at a time. The WHERE clause allows selection of the lines to be updated. The SET clause determines the columns to be updated. The value destined to be assigned to a given column may be a constant, an expression or the result of a sub-query.

Example 7.15
1) Alter the address of client 'Smith'. The new value is '15, The Street'.

```
UPDATE Client
    SET address = '15 The Street'
    WHERE name = 'Smith';
```

2) Increase by 5% the unit prices of products whose price is greater than £100.

```
UPDATE Product
    SET unitprice = unitprice * 1.05
    WHERE unitprice > 100;
```

3) Amend the unit price of product number 123 to that of product number 52.

```
UPDATE Product
    SET unitprice = (SELECT unitprice
                     FROM Product
                     WHERE productid = 52)
    WHERE productid = 123;
```

7.3 Inserting data

Insertion consists of adding new lines to a table. It may affect all columns in a table or only one subset of the columns, in which case the remainder will automatically take null values. Those columns that cannot take null values (that is, those that were NOT NULL when the table was created) must appear in the insert command. The first is as follows:

```
INSERT INTO table [(column,...)]
    VALUES (value,...);
```

This allows the values to be inserted to be shown in the command. If all the columns in the table are affected, it is not necessary to specify them. The list of values in the VALUES clause must correspond to that in the columns to be inserted, both in number and in sequence.

Example 7.16
Add a new product.

```
INSERT INTO Product
VALUES (2121, 'stool', 98, 15);
```

The second form of the insert command allows data to be copied from one table to another. Its syntax is as follows:

```
INSERT INTO table [(column,...)]
    query;
```

Here the lines coming from the selection query are copied into table. As for the first form, there must be a correspondence between the columns of the selection query and those of the table.

Example 7.17
Insert clients from the table Client_london into the table Client.

```
INSERT INTO Client (clientid, name, tel, specterm)
    SELECT *
    FROM Client_london;
```

The remaining columns (address, postcode and town) will take null values.

7.4 Deleting data

Deleting data consists of deleting one or more lines from a table. The command used is DELETE, which has the following syntax:

```
DELETE FROM table
    WHERE condition;
```

The condition allows one to control the lines to be deleted from a table. If no WHERE clause is included, all the lines are deleted. The condition may contain a sub-query. It is not possible to delete some columns in a table and leave others. For this reason, the keyword DELETE may never be followed with the names of columns.

Example 7.18
1) Delete all orders dating from before 28 February 1986.

```
DELETE FROM Order
    WHERE orderdate < '28-feb-86';
```

2) Delete orders placed by client Smith.

```
DELETE FROM Order
   WHERE clientid IN (SELECT clientid
                      FROM Client
                      WHERE name = 'Smith');
```

8 Data Control in SQL

8.1 Management of users and their privileges

8.1.1 Creating and deleting users

In order to access Oracle, a user must be identified as such by the system. To achieve this, he must have a name, a password and a set of privileges. Only the database administrator is empowered to create users. The creation command is as follows:

```
GRANT [CONNECT,] [RESOURCE,] [DBA]
    TO user,...
```

The options CONNECT, RESOURCE and DBA determine which class of user is to be created; that is, the privileges that he may enjoy.

The privileges assigned to these options are:

- connection (CONNECT)
  - log-on to all Oracle tools
  - selection, modification or deletion of data to which access has previously been granted
  - creation of views and synonyms.

It should be noted that a user who has only the privilege to log-on may not create tables, groups or indexes. So a particular user may be restricted to simply manipulating other people's data, without any rights to keeping his own copy or of creating data that is his own.

- creating resources (RESOURCE)

This option only applies to a user who has the CONNECT privilege. It offers him the following additional privileges:

  - creation of tables, indexes and groups
  - attribution of some or all of the privileges on tables, indexes and groups to other users
  - use of the command AUDIT on his own objects.
- administration (DBA : database administrator)

This option encompasses the privileges of the above two options. It offers in addition:
- access to all the data of all users
- creation and deletion of users'privileges
- creation of PUBLIC synonyms
- all the database administration operations (creation/deletion of sectors, saving and restoring the complete database, database control, etc).

A database administrator may also grant a user the facility to connect himself directly without having to mention his password.

The syntax is as follows:

```
GRANT CONNECT
    TO OPS $ <user>
        IDENTIFIED BY pass_word;
```

The IDENTIFIED BY clause is only obligatory when a new user is created or to alter the password of an existing user. It is also possible to create or assign the same privileges to a set of users in one and the same command.

Example 8.1
1) Creation of a new user ac1 with the password 'ac1pwd' with the right of connection only.

```
GRANT CONNECT
    TO ac1
    IDENTIFIED BY ac1pwd;
```

This command may only be executed by users who have the DBA privilege.
2) Allow ac1 to create table and table accelerators.

```
GRANT RESOURCE
    TO ac1;
```

3) Change the password of ac1. The new password is 'ac1pass'.

```
GRANT CONNECT
    TO ac1
    IDENTIFIED BY ac1pass;
```

An Oracle user may be deleted or have certain privileges removed at any time. The necessary command is:

```
REVOKE [CONNECT,] [RESOURCE,] [DBA]
    FROM user,...;
```

The CONNECT option therefore prevents the user from connecting again with Oracle.

8.1.2 Creating and deleting rights

Any table, view or synonym is initially only accessible by the user who created it. In certain cases though, it may be necessary to share objects. To make this possible, Oracle allows the owner of an object to grant privileges on this object to other users. The command for assigning rights has the following syntax:

```
GRANT privilege,...
    ON object
    TO user,...
    [WITH GRANT OPTION];
```

The privileges that may be granted are:

```
SELECT  : select data from tables and views
INSERT  : insert lines in tables or views
UPDATE  : update tables or views
DELETE  : delete lines from tables or views
ALTER   : alter or add to columns in a table
INDEX   : create an index on tables
ALL     : all operations.
```

The privilege on the UPDATE operation may relate only to some columns in a table.

In addition, any user who receives a privilege on a table or view with WITH GRANT OPTION also has the right to grant it to another user.

There is a special user called PUBLIC which means all users.

Example 8.2

Attribute to user ac2 the right to select and update the Client table:

```
GRANT SELECT, UPDATE
    ON Client
    TO ac2;
```

The command to reverse such an assignation goes as follows:

```
REVOKE right,...
    ON object
    FROM user,...;
```

Here too, ALL may be used to designate all privileges and PUBLIC to designate all users.

A privilege may only be withdrawn by the user who granted it or by the database administrator.

Example 8.3
Prevent any operation by any user on the Client table.

```
REVOKE ALL
    ON Client
    FROM PUBLIC;
```

The table is then protected.

8.2 Manipulating data using views

The concept of a view was introduced to allow a user to manipulate data by a means other than via tables defined in the database. A view is a selection of data from one or more tables. It is stored in the form of a select query in the data dictionary. The use of views allows:

- access to be restricted to certain columns or certain lines in a table by only allowing one or more users to manipulate this table via a view
- the user's task to be simplified, since he does not have to formulate complicated queries.

Most operations possible on tables are also possible on views. However, to be usable, a view must first be created.

8.2.1 Creating views

Creating a view consists of defining its schema, that is, its name and those of the columns that go to make it, together with the data that relates to it. The command for creating a view is as follows:

```
CREATE VIEW view [(column,...)]
    AS query
    [WITH CHECK OPTION];
```

The name attributed to a view must be unique and must not relate to any other existing table, view or synonym name. The query allows selection of the columns and lines that will go to make the new view. It may take all the forms of a query that we have met so far. There is however one exception, the GROUP BY clause is not permissible. In addition, it should be noted that the query is not placed within parentheses. It is this that differentiates it from a sub-query. The columns of a view may come from one or more tables. If the names of columns are mentioned after the view name, their number must coincide with that of the columns selected in the query. If no names are specified, the columns of the new view will carry the names of the selected columns. This provides a possible means for renaming the columns of a table.

If the option WITH CHECK OPTION is present, the view may be updated.

Example 8.4

Create a view of the clients in the town of 'Bournemouth'.

```
CREATE VIEW Client_bournemouth
   AS SELECT clientid, name, address, postcode, tel, specterm
   FROM Client
   WHERE town = 'Bournemouth';
```

Once created, a view is affected by all alterations to the tables that go to make it up.

It is possible to rename a view with the same RENAME command as used for tables.

8.2.2 Deleting views

Deleting a view consists of deleting its definition from the data dictionary. The data attached to the view is not deleted. The delete command has the following syntax:

```
DROP VIEW view;
```

8.2.3 Querying using views

All queries that can be made of tables can also be made of views, including use of the GROUP BY clause.

8.2.4 Modifying views

Modifying (updating, deleting and inserting) data in views is subject to certain restrictions. It is not possible to modify all views, especially those that:

- are defined from more than one table
- use an expression or an aggregate function in their definition.

For views that can be modified, the appropriate commands are those used for updating tables, namely DELETE, UPDATE and INSERT.

The Client_bournemouth view may be updated.

9 SQL*Plus Interface

9.1 General introduction

SQL*Plus is an interactive interface that allows the database to be manipulated by means of simple commands based on SQL as described in the previous chapter. In addition, SQL*Plus contains a set of supplementary functions that allow:

- results to be formatted: it is possible to choose the presentation of each column of the result, the size of the page, the title, etc. It is also possible to produce totals by group of lines or for all lines. The result obtained may be displayed on the screen or stored in a file
- help to be obtained: it is possible to obtain help at any time concerning an SQL*Plus command or the description of a table
- control and editing of SQL*Plus commands: SQL*Plus commands may be stored in a file, edited and executed later. They may be parameterised using variables whose values are given by the user at execution
- transaction management: the user may validate or cancel a sequence of update operations
- performance management: it is possible to measure the performance of commands executed by SQL*Plus.

Furthermore, Oracle allows the manipulation of tree-structured data. The manipulation of this structure requires additional clauses to be introduced into the select command. These clauses are not part of SQL but belong to Oracle proper. This is why they have yet to be presented.

9.2 Connecting to SQL*Plus

Connection to SQL*Plus implies that Oracle is already active. At log-on it is possible to specify the user name, password, and the database name:

```
SQLPLUS [user] [/password] [@base]
```

If the user name and/or the password are not given, Oracle asks for them. If no database name is specified, the default database is connected.

The connection may also be made by specifying a command file in the following manner:

```
SQLPLUS @file
```

SQL*Plus will execute the commands contained in the file specified (having the SQL extension). The first line of this file must coincide with a user name followed by a '/' and the password.

In the two preceding cases, it is possible to run SQL*Plus and not connect with a database at all:

```
SQLPLUS / NOLOG
```

Once the connection is established, SQL*Plus will fetch and execute a file called login.sql that contains some parameters for controlling the work environment. This file may be empty, in which case the values of certain parameters take their default values. The command SHOW displays the contents of these parameters.

If the connection is made, SQL*Plus responds with a prompt whose default form is 'SQL>' or the one assigned to the prompt parameter in the login.sql file. The prompt shows that the user may send SQL commands to the database. Each command line begins with the prompt.

The user has two types of assistance available when using SQL*Plus. He can have help with the role and syntax of an SQL or SQL*Plus command. This help is obtained by the HELP command followed by the name of the command in question. If no command name is provided after HELP, all SQL and SQL*Plus commands are displayed.

Example 9.1
The following command gives help with the INSERT command:

```
HELP INSERT;
```

The second type of help that SQL*Plus can offer concerns the description of a given table. By means of the DESCRIBE (or DESC) command, the user can see the structure of the tables that he has been granted privileges on. This description contains the names and column types.

Example 9.2
To list the columns of the Client table, one keys:

```
DESC Client;
```

To conclude, disconnecting from SQL*Plus is carried out with the EXIT command.

9.3 Formatting results

We have seen in the previous chapter that SQL is a powerful language for selecting data from the database. On the other hand, it does not have sufficient facilities for the presentation of the data from the results obtained. A large number of the SQL*Plus commands were introduced to meet that need. A mixture of SQL and SQL*Plus commands makes it possible to produce good quality reports.

The chief SQL*Plus facilities for formatting results are:

- page format
- column format
- breaking sequence
- totalling.

Each format command remains valid until the end of the session, so long as it has not been redefined. It is advisable to place in the login.sql file the format commands that are always required, such as page size and line length.

By default, the result of each query is displayed on the screen and no trace of this result remains. The result can be stored by using the SPOOL command followed by the name of the destination file. From the moment this command is executed, everything that appears on the screen is stored in the file up until the execution of another SPOOL command with the option OFF or OUT. The OUT option causes the contents of a file to be printed.

9.3.1 Formatting a page

Formatting a page consists basically of defining the page size (number of lines per page and number of characters per line) and the text that forms the header and footer of each page.

The definition of the page size is especially useful if one wants to print the result obtained. In this case, the page size must be matched to the paper size with the following commands:

```
SET PAGESIZE n;
SET LINESIZE m;
```

n is the number of lines per page and m the number of characters per line.

To define a top title, the following command must be used: TTITLE [[COL nl SKIP [n] I TAB n I LEFT I RIGHT I CENTER] 'text']...;

The meaning of these different options is:

COL	: align the text from column n (column is used here in the sense of character)
SKIP	: skip n lines before writing the text
TAB	: place the text after n tabulations
LEFT	: left justify
RIGHT	: right justify
CENTER	: centre the text.

Example 9.3

The following command causes each page to begin with a line containing the date on the right and a centred title followed by two skipped lines:

```
TTITLE CENTER 'List of clients' RIGHT '21-02-90' SKIP 2;
```

The definition of a bottom title is made with the BTITLE which has the same syntax as TTITLE.

The following commands turn off the top and bottom titles:

```
TTITLE OFF;
BTITLE OFF;
```

To switch them on again, use the commands:

```
TTITLE ON;
BTITLE ON;
```

9.3.2 Formatting a column

In the absence of any column formatting, SQL*Plus follows a standard display format:

- the name is the column name or an alias defined in the SELECT clause. If this column corresponds to an expression, the expression is displayed
- the width is equal to the size of the column or to the length of the column name if this is greater than the column size.

Formatting a column is done with the COLUMN command whose syntax is:

```
COLUMN column options
```

The options apply to all columns having this name for the entire session. The options defined for one (or all) column(s) can be consulted at any time using the command:

```
COL column;
or COL;
```

The main options used are:

- HEADING string : defines the column name. The spaces in the name are placed between single or double quote marks (' or "). The name may occupy several lines; the I character forces a new line.
- FORMAT mask : determines the format of the contents of the column. There are two types: one for character strings, the other for numbers
  - character format : *An*, where *n* determines the maximum number of characters, that is, the column width (A10 sets the width of a column at 10 characters)
  - numeric formats : there are several numeric formats (see Oracle manuals).
- JUSTIFY L[EFT] I C[ENTER] I R[IGHT] : specifies if the column title is to be aligned on the left, centred or aligned on the right. The default is for the title to be aligned on the left for a character column and on the right for a numeric column.
- WRA[PPED] I WOR[D-WRAPPED] I TRU[NCATED]: specifies if the contents of the column are truncated or continue on the next line if too long for the first.
- NEWLINE : causes line shift before displaying the column.
- NULL string : specifies the string that will be displayed in place of null values (blank is the default).
- PRINT/NOPRINT : specifies if the column is to be displayed or not. PRINT is the default.
- ALIAS name : defines a synonym for the column.
- LIKE column : copies the attributes defined for another column.
- TEMPORARY : the options will only apply to the next SELECT.
- CLEAR : all the options are cancelled.
- DEFAULT : used with other options : options not specified in the COL command take default values. If the DEFAULT option is absent, options not specified in the command retain their old values.
- ON/OFF : allows return to default options while retaining the defined options. These options can be brought back with ON.

Example 9.4
The command:

```
COLUMN qtyord HEADING quantity FORMAT 999;
```

defines the heading of column qtyord and its width.

9.3.3 Output line breaks

SQL*Plus allows the result lines to be grouped according to the values of one or more columns and an action to be carried out at each break in sequence. The lines must be ordered according to the column or columns that serve the break. The appropriate command is:

```
BREAK ON break_element [action]..;
```

The break_element can be:

- a column name : the˙ value in the column is displayed for the first line of the group and it is not repeated for the others.

The action is executed at each change in value of the column

- RAW : the action is executed at each line
- PAGE : the action is executed at each page change
- REPORT : the action is executed at the end of the report.

The action may be:

- SKIP [n] : skip n lines
- PAGE : start a new page.

Example 9.5

Select the orders grouped by client. For each order, give the client identifier, product identifier, quantity ordered, unit price and order value. The break is therefore made on the clientid column.

```
BREAK ON clientid PAGE;
SELECT clientid, productid, qtyord, unitprice, qtyord*unitprice
''total''
FROM Order or, Product pr
WHERE or.productid = pr.productid
ORDER BY clientid;
```

Moving to the next client causes a page to be skipped.

9.3.4 Totalling

The command COMPUTE carries out a calculation on one or more columns each time there is a break on another column. The command:

```
COMPUTE operation OF column1, column2,... ON break_element;
```

causes an additional line to be displayed containing the result of the operation carried out on column1, column2, etc each time there is a break on break_element.

The possible operations are:

- SUM : produce total for each group
- COUNT : count number of lines having a non-null value

- NUMBER : count all lines, even those having a null value
- MIN : find the minimum value in each group
- MAX : find the maximum value in each group
- AVG : find the average in each group
- VAR : calculate the variance in each group
- STD : calculate the deviation in each group.

The break_element has the same meaning as in the command BREAK.

Example 9.6
Returning to the previous example we can insert a command to add the values:

```
COMPUTE SUM OF total ON clientid;
```

9.4 Control and edit commands

9.4.1 Storing SQL and SQL*Plus commands

Each time an SQL command is keyed, it is stored in a buffer area called 'SQL buffer'. So long as another SQL command is not entered, this command remains in the buffer and may therefore be re-executed or edited. However, as soon as another SQL command is entered or the user quits SQL*Plus, the command is lost; hence the need for permanent storage of commands.

The command:

```
SAVE file;
```

stores the contents of the buffer in a file. The SQL extension is added automatically to the file name.

To carry out the reverse operation, that is, copy the contents of a file to the buffer, use the command:

```
GET file;
```

The contents of the file are then copied into the buffer and displayed on the screen, but the command is not executed. To execute the command, either use the RUN command or simply enter the / character.

To load a file and execute it immediately, use the command:

```
START file;
```

The SQL buffer area only stores SQL commands. All the SQL*Plus commands such as those for formatting results are not stored. But SQL*Plus contains a command that allows all commands to be stored, including SQL*Plus commands. It defines another buffer area for this purpose. The command required is:

```
SET BUFFER buffer;
```

Once this command has been used, all new commands are stored in this buffer where they can be edited, executed or copied into a file with the SAVE command.

9.4.2 Editing commands

Capturing and editing commands may be done either by means of the SQL*Plus integral editor, or using a host editor (parameter _EDITOR in the login.sql file). The integral editor offers the following facilities:

- A[PPEND] text : adds text to the end of the current line
- C[HANGE] /old/new : replaces the first occurrence of old by new in the current line
- DEL : deletes the current line
- I[NPUT] : adds lines
- L[IST] [n][m] : lists all lines (if n and m are absent), from n to the end (if m is absent) or from n to m. The last line listed becomes the current line, and it is usually necessary to set the current line to be n, before using A, C or DEL.

9.4.3 Parameterising commands

Given the possibilities described in the previous sections, the reader may be tempted to write 'programs' or 'procedures' that include a set of SQL and SQL*Plus commands. However, an important element is missing in SQL, namely variables. In SQL*PLus there are two ways of achieving this requirement: parameterising and using variables. The two possibilities add a dynamic aspect to SQL commands held in a file since parts of these commands are only evaluated immediately before their execution and may vary from one execution to another.

SQL commands are parameterised by inserting into them parameters instead of constants. These parameters are often used in the WHERE clause of a select command. They prevent a query from being fixed and make it dynamic. A parameter is designated by the & character followed by a digit from 1 to 9. SQL*Plus restricts the number of parameters in an SQL command file to 9 (&1, &2,...&9).

When an SQL command file is activated by the START command, the first parameter (that follows the file name) is assigned to &1, the second to &2, and so on. SQL*Plus displays the lines containing the parameters before and after the substitution. It should however be noted that the use of parameters is not possible with the RUN command.

Example 9.7

List the clients in a town whose name is a variable given during the initiation of the command:

```
SELECT *
FROM CLient
WHERE town = '&1';
```

If this command is stored in the file list_client.sql, to obtain all the London clients we activate it as follows:

```
START list_client London
```

The second way of making SQL commands dynamic is to use variables. A variable is any character string beginning with the & character. The difference between a parameter and a variable lies in the fact that the value of a variable is only requested when the appropriate command is executed. Each time that SQL*Plus finds a variable in a command, it asks the user to give a value that will be assigned to this variable. Another difference compared with parameters is the possibility of using variables in commands executed with both RUN and START.

The command ACCEPT is a more convenient way of entering variable values. It allows the variable type to be defined (numeric or character), displays a message inviting a value to be input and accepts the value input. This value is then automatically assigned to the relevant SQL command.

9.5 Transaction management

SQL*Plus contains the commands COMMIT and ROLLBACK to control the posting and cancellation of transactions:

- COMMIT : verifies the current transaction. Alterations to the database are confirmed and made visible to other users.
- ROLLBACK : cancels the current transaction. The database is restored to its state at the beginning of the transaction.

The default is for any alteration to the database (INSERT, UPDATE or DELETE) only to be verified by the COMMIT command, or when leaving SQL*Plus normally by the use of the EXIT command.

It is possible to place the system in an automatic posting mode, where verification is carried out automatically after each SQL data manipulation command. One of the following commands must be used:

```
SET AUTOCOMMIT IMMEDIATE;
```

or

```
SET AUTOCOMMIT ON;
```

The above is cancelled with the command:

```
SET AUTOCOMMIT OFF;
```

9.6 Performance measurement

The performance of SQL commands initiated under SQL*Plus may be controlled with the following commands:

- TIMING : provides the following information on an SQL command:
  - the elapsed time (ELAPSED)
  - the amount of CPU time taken by the SQL*Plus task (CPU)
  - the number of logical input/outputs or buffer accesses (BUFIO)
  - the number of physical input/outputs or disk accesses (DIRIO)
  - the number of page faults (FAULTS)

  The command:
      SET TIMING {ON|OFF}
  allows alteration of the SQL*Plus variable 'TIMING'.
- CUMUL : it is possible to accumulate the TIMING information for several SQL commands. To achieve this, the information is placed in a so-called 'cumul' zone whose contents are subsequently displayed.

```
TIMING START name_zone
TIMING SHOW
```

The command:

```
TIMING STOP
```

terminates the cumul.

9.7 Manipulation of tree-structured data

Oracle allows tree-structured data to be represented and manipulated. Data is frequently arranged in this way, with objects being made up of other objects, which are in turn made up of other objects, and so on. Two common examples are the hierarchy within an organisation (managing director, board directors, departmental managers, etc) and product classification (a product being made up of a set of other products). In figure 9.1 a living room is seen to contain various elements: non-furniture items, a number of armchairs, a sofa and a coffee table. The non-furniture items may be considered as a group that itself consists of several elements.

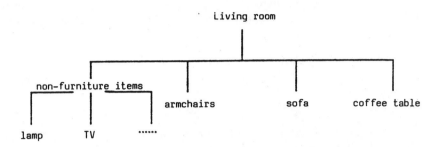

Figure 9.1 Tree structure of a product

At the data definition level, no extension is necessary to represent a tree structure. All data is held in tabular form. To provide for a tree structure possibility, we shall add to the Product table another table called Group that consists of the three columns: group, element and quantity.

To allow manipulation of such tree structures, Oracle has introduced extensions. These are of particular value in searching trees. It is possible to:

– fix the starting point of a search (START WITH)
– choose a direction of search (CONNECT BY PRIOR clause).

Searching upwards is called implosion, while searching downwards is called explosion.

The normal syntax for a search query thus becomes:

```
SELECT columnn,...
FROM table [variable],...
[WHERE condition]
[CONNECT BY [PRIOR] column1 = [PRIOR] column2
[AND condition]
[START WITH condition];
```

The START WITH clause chooses the line(s) used as the starting point for the search of the tree. The condition in this clause includes all the possibilities reviewed in chapter 4 (comparison operators, specific operators: IN, BETWEEN, LIKE, sub-queries, arithmetic expressions, etc).

The CONNECT BY clause sets the direction of the search. To carry out an upward search (implosion), the column containing an element in the tree must be prefixed with the keyword PRIOR. There are therefore two ways of expressing this instruction:

```
CONNECT BY PRIOR element = group
```

and

```
CONNECT BY group = PRIOR element
```

A downwards search (explosion) requires the column containing a set to be prefixed with the keyword **PRIOR**. Again, there are two ways of expressing the instruction:

```
CONNECT BY element = PRIOR group
```

and

```
CONNECT BY PRIOR group = element
```

The difference between the condition in the **WHERE** clause and that in **CONNECT BY** lies in the fact that the first deletes the lines of the result that satisfy this condition, whereas the second deletes the whole branch linked to a line that satisfies this condition.

Example 9.8
Give the list of products that make up product 234:

```
SELECT element, group, quantity
FROM Group
CONNECT BY PRIOR element = group
START WITH group = 234;
```

Oracle allows the nodes of a tree structure to be numbered by means of the concept of **LEVEL**. The root node is level 1, the first sons are level 2, and so on. This numbering may be used to classify the results and especially to give them a clearer presentation. An additional feature available is the **LPAD** function which indents the results.

Example 9.9
To obtain the same list as in the previous example, but with a different display, we could formulate the query as follows:

```
SELECT lpad('', 2*level) | element, group, quantity
FROM Group
CONNECT BY PRIOR element = group
START WITH group = 234;
```

The LPAD function inserts a number of spaces equal to double the level in front of each element in order to show which element belongs to which group.

10 Pro*C Precompiler

10.1 Introduction

The main characteristic of SQL is its non-procedural aspect. The user does not have to specify how to obtain data but simply what data he wants. Of course, this greatly simplifies the user's task, but on the other hand it deprives him of the other advantages of more conventional programming languages, such as repeat, condition and choice from alternatives. These features prove necessary in practice, particularly in applications that are strongly based on algorithms.

The solution adopted in Oracle to overcome this problem is to combine the non-procedural character of SQL with the facilities of a high level language. It thus becomes possible to insert SQL commands into a program written in COBOL, C or Fortran. A defining or data-manipulating command in SQL can thus be executed if a particular condition is verified or repeated a certain number of times. A choice can also be made from several SQL commands.

Oracle contains two large families of tools for this purpose. The first consists of a set of modules that can be called from a program in order to access an Oracle database. This set of modules is known as an Oracle Call Interface (OCI). To connect to Oracle or execute any SQL command necessitates calling the corresponding module with the appropriate parameters. Then, after the program is compiled, editing the links is done with a library containing the interface modules. This library is currently available with the languages COBOL, C and Fortran. The main disadvantage of these interfaces lies in the inflexible way that modules are called. Each module has a set of parameters whose order and data types must be respected. The second family of tools consists of precompilers called Pro*Language, where 'Language' is the name of the corresponding programming language, called the host language in all that follows. Use of these precompilers overcomes the inconvenience of the OCI by making it possible to insert SQL commands directly in the program. Writing programs thus becomes more flexible since there is no longer any direct call to external modules.

The precompilers currently available cover most existing languages; for example, Pro*COBOL, Pro*C, Pro*Fortran, Pro*Pascal and Pro*PL/1. The choice of a particular precompiler depends on the application. Usually, management applications use Pro*COBOL while Pro*Fortran is used for scientific applications.

In this chapter we will concentrate on the second family of tools, in particular the Pro*C precompiler. After a general introduction, we will tackle the elements of writing Pro*C programs one by one. In section 10.3 we will discuss the declarative part of the program, while 10.4 and 10.5 deal with the executive part. Only a minimum knowledge of C is required.

10.2 Overview of Pro*C

The role of the Pro*C precompiler is to translate a program including SQL commands into a program that only includes instructions in C capable of accessing the database to carry out required operations. It consists basically of replacing SQL commands with calls to OCI Oracle modules. For convenience, we will refer to programs containing SQL instructions that are to be handled by the Pro*C precompiler as Pro*C programs, by analogy with C programs.

The Pro*C tool consists mainly of:
– precompiler software
– libraries used to communicate with Oracle.

The libraries vary according to the programming environment. On a PC, for example, there are two libraries: SQLLC.LIB for the Lattice C compiler, and SQLMSC.LIB for the Microsoft C compiler.

Writing a program in Pro*C is done in the following steps:
1) Write the program in Pro*C consisting of C instructions and SQL commands. The source file containing this program must have a special extension. Under VMS, Unix and MS-DOS this extension is 'pc'.
2) Precompile this program with the following command:

```
PCC INAME = source [HOST = language] [option = value...]
```

The INAME indicates the name of the source file. If the name of the source file is given with its extension, the HOST argument may be omitted. If not, the HOST argument must be present, because it shows the host language in use (C in this case).

The options determine some of the precompiler parameters. The Oracle manuals contain a list of these options, together with the values that may be assigned to them.

If there are no errors, the result of this stage is a file that has the same name as the source file but with the extension 'c'. It contains a purely C program in which all the SQL commands have been substituted with calls to modules in the Oracle library. Data structures are also added to the source program.

3) Compile the C program. If there are no errors, an object file is generated.
4) Edit object file links using the appropriate library (SQLMSC.LIB in the Microsoft C environment). If no error is found, an executable file is then generated.

A Pro*C program consists of two parts: a declarative part and an executable part. The first allows variable to be declared by means of which data is exchanged between the SQL commands and the C instructions. It also allows a communication zone to be declared that is used in particular for error control and control of the sequence of SQL commands. The second part is made up of the body of the program; it contains instructions executable in C and in SQL.

Figure 10.1 shows the interaction between an application program containing SQL commands and Oracle. This interaction takes places via OCI modules that translate SQL commands, the communication zone and another buffer zone called cursor. The latter is used in select queries.

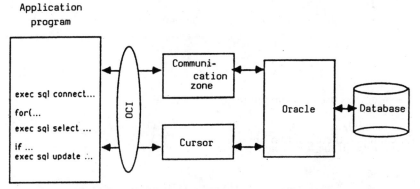

Figure 10.1 Interaction between an application program and Oracle

10.3 Declarative part of a Pro*C program

This part declares first the variables that may be used in SQL instructions and then the communication zone with Oracle.

10.3.1 Variable declaration

The declaration of variables is done in a zone defined by the following two instructions:

```
EXEC SQL BEGIN DECLARE SECTION;
EXEC SQL END DECLARE SECTION;
```

Two types of variable can be declared between these instructions: host variables and indicators.

Host variables are variables that will be used in the body of the program by SQL instructions in the same way as constants in interactive SQL. The declaration of these variables follows the same rules as for declaring variables in C.

The host variables may then be used in the program like any variables declared in the body of the program, except that they must be prefixed by ':' when they are used in SQL commands.

Pro*C introduces an additional type (or pseudo type) of data which is the VARCHAR type. It describes character strings of variable length. Declaration of a variable of this type is equivalent to declaring a structure that has the same name as the variable and is made up of a field that will contain the length of the string and a second field that will contain the string itself.

Example 10.1
If we wish to find the name, address, postcode and town of a client, given his number, we shall need to declare the following variables:

```
EXEC SQL BEGIN DECLARE SECTION;
      char client_id[6];
      varchar client_name[20];
      client_address[40];
      int post_code;
      varchar town[10];
EXEC SQL END DECLARE SECTION;
```

The VARCHAR declaration client_name[20] is equivalent to a declaration of the following structure:

```
struct {
       unsigned short int len;/*length of string*/
       unsigned char arr[40];/*array of characters*/
       }client_name;
```

When the variable 'client_name' is used as an input variable, the field 'len' must be initialised with the length of the string assigned to 'arr'. Outside of SQL commands, the variable 'client-name' may not be used directly. Its components 'len' and 'arr' have to be manipulated in the same way as the elements of a structure, that is, by designating them respectively by 'client_name.len' and 'client_name.arr'. On the other hand, in SQL commands the variable 'client_name' has to be used.

The second type of variable that may be declared is indicators. These are optional variables that are used in parallel with host variables. There is an indicator for each host variable. Indicators are used to manipulate null values when consulting or updating data and to give information about the execution of an SQL command. They may be of type 'short' or 'short int'. When used in a program they follow the same rules as those for host variables with the additional constraint that an indicator must always be preceded by its corresponding host variable in SQL commands.

After execution of an SQL command, the value of an indicator associated with a host variable is:

0 if the variable has received a non-null and non-truncated value
−1 if the variable has received a null value (NULL)
n (>0) if the value assigned to the variable has been truncated. n indicates the size of the value before truncation.

Example 10.2

Suppose that after finding the name, address, postcode and town of a client, we only want to display the result if the address is complete (no null values for the address, postcode and town columns). To identify the columns with a null value, indicators will have to be used. The declaration part then becomes:

```
EXEC SQL BEGIN DECLARE SECTION;
        char client_id[6];
        varchar client_name[20];
        client_address[40];
        int post_code;
        varchar town[10];
        short int ind_addr, ind_code, ind_town;
EXEC SQL END DECLARE SECTION;
```

The indicators defined in this example may also be used to check if the values assigned to the host variables have not been truncated because of a mismatch in the sizes of the columns in the Client table of the database compared with the variables defined in the program.

10.3.2 Declaration of communication zone

The communication zone is a set of variables predefined by Pro*C. Its role is to provide communication between the program and Oracle when SQL commands are executed. After execution of an SQL command, the contents of the variables in this zone provide diagnostic evidence of this execution. One can see whether or not there was an error, what it was, the number of lines affected by the command, etc.

Discovery of any errors will allow other action to be taken. This is all the more useful given that an error, on executing an SQL command, does not prevent the program from continuing if no such precautions have been taken (see the WHENEVER command). As we have shown above, the communication zone is a set of predefined variables. These are contained in a file called SQLCA.H which has to be included in the program. To do this, the following command is added to the program after the section dealing with the declaration of host variables:

```
EXEC SQL INCLUDE SQLCA;
```

The SQLCA.H file is basically made up of a structure also called sqlca, whose chief variables are:

sqlcode : contains a return code indicating how the last SQL command was executed
sqlerrm.sqlerrmc : contains the error message
sqlerrd : is a six-element array. The third element (sqlerrd[2]) contains the number of lines that were involved by the SQL command
sqlwarn : is an eight-element array indicating 'warnings' during execution.

For a complete description of the variables in the communication zone, the reader is advised to consult the Oracle manuals.

10.4 Data definition and simple manipulation in Pro*C

Once the host variables and those of the communication zone have been defined, we come to the executive part of a Pro*C program. The first command of this part must always be the one that ensures connection with Oracle. Then come those that allow access to data, such as selection, alteration, deletion or insertion. Process units, or transactions, may also be defined, validated or cancelled. As for error handling, it is used to control the processing of simple commands.

10.4.1 Connecting with Oracle

To access data, one must first be connected to Oracle by means of a user name and password. As in SQL*PLus and other Oracle tools, this connection may be made in two ways: either by giving both the user name and password separated by '/', or by giving them separately. The two relevant commands are:

```
EXEC SQL CONNECT :user_id;   or
EXEC SQL CONNECT ;user_name
IDENTIFIED BY :password;
```

In the first form, the host variable user_id must contain the user name followed by a '/' and the password (for example, 'ac1/ac1psw').

In the second form, the first host variable user_name contains the user name, and the second ('password') contains the password (for example, 'ac1' and 'ac1psw').

The user name and the password may be included directly in the program or introduced during execution and then assigned to the appropriate variables. The second solution is preferable because it is more secure and does not require programs to be altered when a user changes his password.

As for disconnecting from Oracle, this occurs automatically when the program stops. It is possible to disconnect before the end of the program by using the RELEASE option in the COMMIT WORK or ROLLBACK WORK commands. We shall return to these two commands in section 10.4.6.

Example 10.3
The following program requests the user name and password and ensures connection with Oracle under this name and password.

```
#include <stdio.h>
EXEC SQL BEGIN DECLARE SECTION;
      varchar us_name[20];
      varchar password[20];
      EXEC SQL END DECLARE SECTION;
      EXEC SQL INCLUDE SQLCA;
      Connection()
      {
            printf("Your name : ");
            scanf("%s", us_name.arr);
            us_name.len=strlen(us_name.arr);
            printf("\nYour password :");
            scanf("%s", password.arr);
            password.len=strlen(password.arr);
            EXEC SQL WHENEVER SQLERROR GOTO ERROR;
            EXEC SQL CONNECT :us_name identified by :password;
            printf("connection to Oracle made. \n");
            return(0);
      Error :
            printf("Error :%s \n", sqlca.sqlerrm.sqlerrmc);
            return(-1);
      }
```

Notes
(i) The WHENEVER command allows errors to be handled. We return to this topic in 10.4.5.
(ii) The program is in fact a function that returns the value 0 if the connection is made and −1 if not. In all the examples that follow in this chapter, we shall refer to this function for connecting with Oracle.

10.4.2 Data definition

In a Pro*C program it is possible to include SQL commands to define data, such as the creation or deletion of a table or view, alteration of a table structure, and so on. This is especially useful when using Oracle's facilities for storing intermediate data. In such a case, temporary tables are created that will be deleted after the necessary manipulations have been made.

The syntax of commands for defining data is the same as in SQL except that they are prefixed with EXEC SQL.

Example 10.4

Create a table Temp_client with the same schema as the Client table of our example database.

```
EXEC SQL CREATE TABLE Temp_client
        (clientid char(6) NOT NULL, name char(20), address
        char(40), postcode number(5), town char(10),
        tel number(8), specterm char(20));
```

To delete this table, this command is required:

```
EXEC SQL DROP TABLE Temp_client;
```

10.4.3 Simple data selection

What we here understand by simple selection is a command that results in zero or a line. Commands whose result consists of more than one line are discussed in 10.4.5.

The conclusion of any query is the return of one or more lines that constitute the result. In interactive SQL (SQL*Plus) the results are displayed directly or the screen or sent to a buffer file (spooler). Now the aim of Pro*C is to recover these results for further processing. These results will be stored in an intermediate zone. This constraint requires the introduction of host variables and an additional clause in the selection commands: the INTO clause.

So, in addition to the normal clauses (SELECT, FROM, WHERE, GROUP BY and HAVING), a query may have an INTO clause. The start of a selection command then appears as:

```
SELECT column,.. INTO :host_variable [ :indicator],...
```

The number of host variables must correspond to the number of columns or clauses in the SELECT clause. Values are assigned in the same order as given in the query, that is, the first column will be assigned to the first variable and so on. Where present, indicators will show if the corresponding column contains a null value or a value that cannot be held in its entirety in the assigned variable (truncation).

Host variables are not only usable in the INTO clause; they may appear anywhere that a constant is usable (WHERE, SET clause).

Example 10.5
Taking example 10.2 let us suppose that the client number is given during program execution.

```
#include <stdio.h
EXEC SQL BEGIN DECLARE SECTION;
      char client_id[6];
      varchar client_name[20];
      client_address[40];
      int postcode;
      varchar town[10];
      short int ind_addr, ind_code, ind_town;
EXEC SQL END DECLARE SECTION;
EXEC SQL INCLUDE SQLCA;
main()
{
      if(connection() < 0) stop; /* connection to Oracle*/
      printf("Give client number :");
      scanf("%s, client_id.arr);
      client_id.len=strlen(client_id.arr);
      EXEC SQL WHENEVER NOT FOUND GOTO nonexistent;
      EXEC SQL SELECT name, address, postcode, town
                  INTO :client_name, :client_addr:ind_addr,
                      :post_code:ind_code, :town:ind_town
                  FROM Client
                  WHERE clientid = :client_id;
      if ((ind_addr == -1) | (ind_code == -1) | (ind_town == -1))
      /* at least one of the three columns has a null value*/
      printf("Address incomplete for client %s\n", client_name);
      else
          {
          printf("\nName :%s", client_name);
          printf("\nAddress ;%s", client_addr);
          printf("\n\t\t %d %s \n", post_code, town);
          }
      exit(0);
nonexistent :
```

```
        printf("Client nonexistent. \n");
        exit(-1);
  }
```

The **WHENEVER** line identifies the case where there is no client with the number supplied.

10.4.4 *Updating data*

All SQL commands for updating data may be used in Pro*C. The only difference is that host variables may also be used.

Example 10.6
This program alters the telephone number of a client whose identification number is given by the user during execution.

```
#include <stdio.h>
EXEC SQL BEGIN DECLARE SECTION;
     char client_id[6];
     int tel;
     short int ind_tel;
EXEC SQL END DECLARE SECTION;
EXEC SQL INCLUDE SQLCA;
main()
{
     int ret;
     if (connection() < 0) stop; /* connection to Oracle */
     printf("\nClient number :");
     scanf("%s, client_id);
     printf("\nNew telephone number :");
     ret = scanf("%d", tel);
     if (ret == EOF | ret == 0)
     /* if no value is given insert a null value */
     ind_tel = -1;
     else ind_tel = 0;
     EXEC SQL UPDATE Client
             SET tel = :tel
             WHERE clientid = :client_id;
  }
```

10.4.5 Error handling

During precompiling of a program, Pro*C does not carry out an exhaustive checking of SQL commands. Error in syntax or semantics may persist and will therefore not be detected at program execution. Detection of such errors provokes no action and the program continues, unless the programmer has already provided for error handling or a fatal error occurs.

In Pro*C error handling can occur in two ways. The first consists of consulting the indicators and the contents of the communication zone after execution of an SQL command and undertaking the appropriate operations depending on their values. The second calls specific instructions provided in Pro*C for this purpose. The first method is more tedious, but offers greater possibilities. The second is easier to use but less precise and covers fewer cases. Sometimes it may even lead to unexpected results if badly used. The two methods are not incompatible and may be used jointly, which is probably the most effective way.

Using the communication zone and indicators

The communication zone is made up of a set of variables whose contents are altered after execution of every SQL command. By consulting these variables it is possible to gain information about the performance of the previous command and so take any necessary action. In what follows we will consider some of these variables and give possible values that they may have after execution of an SQL command. Other variables are used much less frequently. Full information may be obtained from the Oracle manuals.

- The variable sqlcode : contains a number that shows how the command has been executed. It may have the following values:
  - zero : no error
  - a positive number : return code for no error. The only code used in the current version (V1.1) is 1403 which indicates that no line satisfies the condition mentioned or that the final line has been selected
  - a negative number : error code (see Oracle manuals for the complete list).
- The variable sqlerrm.sqlerrmc : contains the message relating to the error shown in sqlcode.
- The variable sqlerrm.sqlerrml : contains the length of the message contained in sqlerrm.sqlerrmc.
- The variable sqlerrd[2] : contains the number of lines selected, deleted or modified.
- The variable sqlwarn[0] : contains the character 'W' if at least one of the other elements in this table has the value 'W'.

- The variable sqlwarn[1] : contains the character 'W' if one of the values returned in a host variable is truncated. To know which, the indicators of the host variables must be consulted.
- The value sqlwarn[3] : contains the character 'W' if the number of host variables in the INTO clause does not correspond to the number of columns in the SELECT clause.

Checking the indicators after execution of a command may give additional information about the state of host variables. This information complements that given by the variables in the communication zone.

Using the WHENEVER command

Pro*C contains a command that detects errors which occur during execution and takes appropriate action. It is a kind of trigger (see chapter 11) for which the triggering event is a particular error or type of error and where the remedial action is provided for by the programmer. The two components of this command are thus the triggering event and the action. The syntax for this is:

```
EXEC SQL WHENEVER <event> <action>;
```

The possible events are:

- SQLERROR : if any error occurs (sqlca.sqlcode < 0)
- SQLWARNING : if any warning occurs (sqlca.sqlwarn[0] = 'W')
- NOT FOUND : if any line does not satisfy the condition (sqlca.sqlcode = 1403).

The actions that may be taken are:

- STOP : causes the program to halt immediately and the operations carried out in the processor are cancelled (see 10.4.6)
- CONTINUE : does not take the error into account and continues program execution
- GO TO <label> : jump to the instruction that follows the label given.

Notes

(i) When it is defined, a WHENEVER command remains valid for all SQL commands encountered up to the next WHENEVER command given. Therefore, it should be used with care and redefined if the error handling is not the same for several SQL commands.

(ii) During precompiling, this command is replaced with the corresponding code wherever it appears. As a consequence its field of application is determined by its physical location in the program and not by the program logic.

Most of the examples in this chapter deal with error cases.

10.4.6 Transaction management

As in interactive SQL, it is possible to define logical processing units (or transactions) in a Pro*C program. We recall that a transaction is a set of commands that only have any meaning if they are all executed. This concept guarantees the coherence and integrity of data.

The first executable SQL command apart from the one that connects with Oracle represents the implicit start of a transaction. The implicit end is marked by the stopping of the program. Between these two points, the programmer may divide the program up into logical units depending on the constraints of the database and the risks of error during execution. There are two commands for the confirmation and cancellation of operations carried out in the current transaction. Each of these terminates a process unit and marks the beginning of another.

The command COMMIT verifies a transaction, that is, it confirms the updates already made. The syntax is:

```
EXEC SQL COMMIT WORK [RELEASE];
```

The RELEASE option frees the resources and disconnects from Oracle. It is advisable to use it as often as possible in the program in order to avoid any unnecessary blockage of resources and delay to other users (processes).

It should be noted that the COMMIT command may be used with the RELEASE option to free resources or disconnect from Oracle.

Data definition commands are verified automatically. In addition, before execution of a data definition command, the preceding process unit is also verified automatically even if the data definition command fails. The ROLL-BACK command cancels the operations of the current transaction. The database then reassumes its state prior to the transaction using the before image file. The syntax of this command is:

```
EXEC SQL ROLLBACK WORK [RELEASE];
```

The RELEASE option has the same effect as in the COMMIT command.

This command is generally used in a function or part of the program called in the case of an error. As with any command, it may also fail and will then call upon the same function or part of the program, causing an infinite loop. To avoid such an eventuality, the ROLLBACK command is prefixed with a command such as:

```
EXEC SQL WHENEVER SQLERROR CONTINUE;
```

Example 10.7
Alter the number of a client in the Client table and in all the orders relating to this client in the Order table.

```
#include <stdio.h>
EXEC SQL BEGIN DECLARE SECTION;
      char old_id[6], new_id[6];
EXEC SQL END DECLARE SECTION;
EXEC SQL INCLUDE SQLCA;
main()
{
      if(connection() < 0) stop; /* connection to Oracle */
      printf("\nGive the old then the new client number : ");
      scanf("%s%s", old_id, new_id);
      EXEC SQL WHENEVER SQLERROR GOTO cancel;
      EXEC SQL UPDATE Client
              SET clientid = :new_id
              WHERE clientid = :old_id;
      EXEC SQL UPDATE Order
              SET clientid = :new_id
              WHERE clientid = :old_id;
      printf("\n%d lines altered in the Order table. \n",
      sqlca.sqlerrd[2]);
      EXEC SQL COMMIT WORK RELEASE;
      exit(0);
cancel :
      printf("Error : %s\n", sqlca.sqlerrm.sqlerrmc);
      EXEC SQL WHENEVER SQLERROR CONTINUE;
      EXEC SQL ROLLBACK WORK RELEASE;
      exit(-1);
}
```

10.5 Queries returning a set of lines

Up until now, we have only dealt with queries that provide a result in a single line. But this is far from the most frequent case in practice. Generally, a query returns a set of lines whose number is unknown before execution. Pro*C has two solutions for handling this. The first is by using arrays of host variables to hold all the result lines. The second uses a work zone called cursor that allows selection one by one of the lines that satisify a given condition (by assigning values to the host variables). The following sections discuss each of these solutions.

10.5.1 *Using host variable arrays*

When an SQL selection command uses simple host variables in the INTO clause and there is more than one line in the database that satisfies the condition of this command, Oracle displays an error message indicating that the command returns more than one line. This type of error can be avoided by using array type host variables, provided that the size of the array is at least equal to the number of lines returned.

Array type host variables are declared in the same way as simple variables but giving their size in addition. If several are to be used in the same INTO clause, they must be the same size. On execution of the command, the values in each column selected will be assigned to the elements in the corresponding array.

If we take t to be the size of the host variable arrays used in the INTO clause, and n the number of lines selected, we find: if n <= t the elements remaining in the array are unaltered, if n > t only the t first lines are selected.

Re-executing the command still gives the first t columns, not the subsequent columns. We note therefore that this method is of little practical value, especially when the programmer has no idea of the number of lines that will be selected. He will have to choose between wasting memory space owing to the allocation of huge arrays or obtaining incomplete results.

Finally, we should note that it is not possible to use array type host variables in the WHERE clause of a selection command.

Example 10.8
Select the designation and unit price of the ten cheapest products.

```
#include <stdio.h>
EXEC SQL BEGIN DECLARE SECTION;
      char design[10][20];
      int price[10];
EXEC SQL END DECLARE SECTION;
EXEC SQL INCLUDE SQLCA;
main()
{
      if (connection() < 0) stop; /* connection to Oracle*/
      EXEC SQL WHENEVER SQLERROR GOTO error;
      EXEC SQL SELECT designation, unitprice
              INTO :design, :price
              FROM Product
              ORDER BY unitprice;
          /* Display results */
```

```
          :
          :
          :
      exit(0);
error :
          printf("Error ; %s\n", sqlca.sqlerrm.sqlerrmc);
          exit(-1);
}
```

Array type host variables may also be used in commands for inserting and modifying data. In this case, each array must be initialised with the values to be inserted or altered. The following rules should be obeyed:

- The arrays used in the VALUES clause of an insertion column must be of the same size.
- It is not possible to use both simple variables and array type variables within the same modification command. The WHERE clause must therefore also use array type variables.

A modification command such as:

```
EXEC SQL UPDATE table
SET column = :var1
WHERE expression = :var2;
```

where var1 and var2 are array type host variables is equivalent to a loop that repeats the following command:

```
EXEC SQL UPDATE table
SET column = :var1[i]
WHERE expression = :var2[i];
```

The use of arrays of host variables in insertion or modification commands is particularly valuable when the source data comes from a file.

10.5.2 Using the cursor

This second solution consists of defining a storage zone whose size is fixed dynamically during execution of the program and which will contain all the selected lines. This zone is called cursor. It allows more than one line to be selected without the actual number of lines selected being known in advance.

A cursor is assigned to a query. In the same program there may be as many cursors as there are queries, but all of these cursors must have distinctive names. The maximum number of cursors possible in a program can be fixed during the calling of the precompiler using the option MAXOPENCURSORS (see 10.2).

The following steps are required to use the cursor:

- define cursor
- open cursor
- search cursor
- close cursor.

Defining the cursor
Defining the cursor consists of assigning it a name and a query. The syntax of this definition is thus:

```
EXEC SQL DECLARE cursor_name CURSOR FOR query;
```

The name chosen in the definition will be used each time that reference is made to this cursor. As for the query, it has the same syntax as in SQL. It may contain host variables. The INTO clause is not necessary here.

Example 10.9
Give the list of products whose price does not exceed a value given during the execution of the program (the variable is ceiling).

```
EXEC SQL DECLARE crs CURSOR FOR
        SELECT designation, unitprice
        FROM Product
        WHERE unitprice <= :ceiling;
```

Opening the cursor
The command for defining the cursor is a declarative command and therefore does not cause the corresponding query to be executed. The cursor has to be 'opened' for the command to be evaluated. The lines that will form the result are identified but they are not yet returned. Any alteration of the host variables that may be used in the WHERE clause after the cursor is opened has no effect on the result. The cursor opening command takes the following form:

```
EXEC SQL OPEN cursor_name;
```

Searching the cursor
After the cursor is opened, the selected lines are available and may be assigned to the host variables. The following command then allows a line to be fetched and its values assigned to the host variables:

```
EXEC SQL FETCH cursor_name INTO :host_variable,...;
```

The number of host variables must correspond to the number of columns in the SELECT clause of the query defined in the DECLARE CURSOR command.

The first execution of the FETCH command returns the first cursor line. Then, each subsequent execution gives the next line until the last line is reached. If another attempt to execute is made, an error is triggered (code 1403).

Closing the cursor

When the search is finished, the cursor must be closed. Closure then frees the corresponding zone. The command to close the cursor is:

```
EXEC SQL CLOSE cursor_name;
```

Example 10.10

Here is the complete program using the cursor defined in example 10.9.

```
#include <stdio.h>
EXEC SQL BEGIN DECLARE SECTION;
    char design[20];
    int price, ceiling;
EXEC SQL DECLARE SECTION;
EXEC SQL INCLUDE SQLCA;
main()
{
    if (connection() < 0) stop; /* connection to Oracle*/
    printf("Give the ceiling price : ");
    scanf("%d n", &ceiling);
    EXEC SQL WHENEVER SQLERROR GOTO error;
    EXEC SQL DECLARE crs CURSOR FOR
             SELECT designation, unitprice
             FROM Product
             WHERE unitprice <= :ceiling;
    EXEC SQL OPEN crs;
    EXEC SQL WHENEVER NOT FOUND GOTO remainder;
    while (1)
             {
             EXEC SQL FETCH Crs INTO :design, :price;
             printf("\n%s\t%d", design, price);
             }
remainder :
    EXEC SQL CLOSE crs;
    EXEC SQL WHENEVER SQLERROR CONTINUE;


    EXEC SQL COMMIT WORK RELEASE;
    exit(0);
error :
```

```
    printf("R.Error : %s. \n", sqlca.sqlerrm.sqlerrmc);
    EXEC SQL WHENEVER SQLERROR CONTINUE;
    EXEC SQL ROLLBACK WORK RELEASE;
    exit(-1);
}
```

10.6 Dynamic commands

All the commands discussed in the preceding sections are known as soon as
the program is written. The user can only intervene at the level of the
values acquired by the host variables. These are static commands, because
the programmer knows which tables and which columns will be manipulated.
In certain cases, these tables and/or columns may not be known when the
program is written. They are fixed by the user when the program is
executed. The choice of entering the whole of the command or part of it,
such as the condition for the selection, may be left to the user. This second
type of command is called a dynamic command. Thus, the definition of a
dynamic command is a command that is not completely known during
compilation of the program.

Pro*C allows a complete SQL command to be entered during execution
of the program or one to be constructed from 'bits' given by the user. This
second possibility is especially useful for users unfamiliar with SQL. An
SQL command can be constructed by gathering together elements of user
responses to questions asked.

We distinguish four circumstances for formulating dynamic commands:

- immediate execution (EXECUTE IMMEDIATE)
- preparation then execution (PREPARE and EXECUTE)
- preparation then cursor use (PREPARE and FETCH)
- use of descriptors.

10.6.1 First circumstance: immediate execution

The command can be given in its totality by the user or only be completed
by him. It is then stored in a host variable and executed with the EXECUTE
IMMEDIATE command whose syntax is:

```
    EXEC SQL EXECUTE IMMEDIATE :host_variable_str;
```

The host variable is a character string type and of sufficient length to
contain the command. It must be declared in the declaration section.

It should be noted that the command given by the user must not begin
with EXEC SQL.

In this first form, the command contained in the host variable:

- may not be a selection command
- may not have host variables
- may not be executed more than once.

Example 10.11

Delete those products that verify the condition chosen by the user.

```
#include <stdio.h>
EXEC SQL BEGIN DECLARE SECTION;
     char condition[50];
     char command[100];
EXEC SQL END DECLARE SECTION;
EXEC SQL INCLUDE SQLCA:
main()
{
     if (connection() < 0) stop; /* connection to Oracle */
     strcpy(command, "delete from product where");
      printf("Give condition to be satisfied for product to be
deleted :");
     scanf("%s n", condition);
     strcat(command, condition);
     EXEC SQL WHENEVER SQLERROR GOTO error;
     EXEC SQL EXECUTE IMMEDIATE :command;
     EXEC SQL COMMIT WORK RELEASE;
     exit(0);
error :
     printf("Error : %S.\n", sqlca.sqlerrm.sqlerrmc);
     EXEC SQL WHENEVER SQLERROR CONTINUE;
     EXEC SQL ROLLBACK WORK RELEASE;
     exit(-1);
}
```

10.6.2 Second circumstance: preparation then execution

The command entered by the user or constructed in the program is first prepared, then executed. The command is initially stored in a host variable as in the first form.

The preparation consists of formulating the command and giving it a name (as for a cursor). This is done with the following command:

```
EXEC SQL PREPARE name FROM :host_variable_str;
```

The name is the one assigned to the command to be executed and host_variable_str is the name of the variable containing this command.

In this second form, it is possible to use host variables in the command.

The execution command has the following syntax:

```
EXEC SQL EXECUTE name [USING :host_variable,...]:
```

The USING clause is only obligatory if the command contains host variables. A command may here be executed several times in contrast to the commands of the first form. The result of each execution varies if the contents of the host variables assigned to the command vary. But as with the first form, this second form does not apply to selection commands.

Example 10.12

Execution of a command containing a host variable. The command and the value of the host variable are given during execution.

```
#include <stdio.h>
EXEC SQL BEGIN DECLARE SECTION;
     char value[20];
     char command[100];
EXEC SQL END DECLARE SECTION;
EXEC SQL INCLUDE SQLCA;
main()
{
     if (connection() < 0) stop; /* connection to Oracle */
     printf("Give command to be executed :");
     scanf("%s n", command);
     EXEC SQL WHENEVER SQLERROR GOTO error;
     EXEC SQL PREPARE com FROM :command;
     printf("Give value of host variable (END to finish :");
     scanf("%s n", value);
     while (strcmp(value, "END") != 0)
             {
                  EXEC SQL EXECUTE com USING :value:
                  scanf("%s n", value);
             }
     EXEC SQL COMMIT WORK RELEASE;
     exit(0);
error :
     printf("Error :%s.\n", sqlca.sqlerrm.sqlerrmc);
     EXEC SQL WHENEVER SQLERROR CONTINUE;
     EXEC SQL ROLLBACK WORK RELEASE;
     exit(-1);
}
```

10.6.3 Third circumstance: use of the cursor

This may apply to selection commands whose list of columns to be selected is known when the program is written. The other clauses, and especially the WHERE clause, can be fixed by the user. This form uses the cursors and it does so in five stages:

a) Preparation as in the preceding form:
   EXEC SQL PREPARE command_name FROM :host_variable_str;
   where host_variable_str is the character string containing the query to be executed. Remember that the INTO clause is not necessary in this case.

b) Cursor definition:
   EXEC SQL DECLARE cursor_name CURSOR FOR command_name;
   where command_name is the one chosen in the PREPARE command.

c) Opening the cursor:
   EXEC SQL OPEN cursor_name [USING :host_variable,...];
   The USING clause is used only when the query contains host variables. The number of host variables in the command must correspond to the number of host variables in this clause.

d) Search:
   EXEC SQL FETCH cursor_name INTO :host_variable,...;
   The host variables of the INTO clause are those that are to receive the result of the search.

e) Closing the cursor:
   EXEC SQL CLOSE cursor_name;

Example 10.13
Find the designation and the unit price of products that satisfy a condition given during execution.

```
#include <stdio.h>
EXEC SQL BEGIN DECLARE SECTION;
      char design[20];
      int price;
      char command[100], condition[50];
EXEC SQL END DECLARE SECTION;
EXEC SQL INCLUDE SQLCA:
main()
```

```
{
      if (connection() < 0) stop; /* connection to Oracle */
      strcpy(command, "select designation, unitprice from product
where");
      printf("Give the condition to be satisfied for the following
query :%s:", command);
      scanf("%s", condition);
      strcat(command, condition);
      EXEC SQL WHENEVER SQLERROR GOTO error;
      EXEC SQL PREPARE com FROM command;
      EXEC SQL DECLARE crs CURSOR FOR com;
      EXEC SQL OPEN crs;
      EXEC SQL WHENEVER NOT FOUND STOP;
      while (1)
               {
                  EXEC SQL FETCH crs INTO :design, :price;
                  printf("\n%s \t%d", design, price);
               }
      EXEC SQL CLOSE crs;

         EXEC SQL WHENEVER SQLERROR CONTINUE;
      EXEC SQL COMMIT WORK RELEASE;
      exit(0);
   error :
      printf("Error : %s.\n", sqlca.sqlerrm.sqlerrmc);
      EXEC SQL WHENEVER SQLERROR CONTINUE;
      EXEC SQL ROLLBACK WORK RELEASE;
      EXIT(-1);
}
```

10.6.4 *Fourth circumstance: use of descriptors*

This last circumstance deals with the most usual case, that is, queries where the list of columns to be selected and the selection criteria are not known when the program is written. To be able to treat this general case, a descriptor zone is used, called SQLDA (SQL Descriptor Area), which is reached with the aid of the DESCRIBE command. The role of this zone is similar to that of the SQLCA zone since it allows communication between the program and Oracle (in so far as the dynamic aspect of commands is concerned).

The role of the DESCRIBE command is to analyse the query input during program execution and to determine the number and type of the columns to be selected. A detailed description of the SQLDA zone and its use is given in the Oracle manuals.

11 Form-driven Screen Display: SQL*Forms

11.1 Introduction

SQL*Forms is an interactive tool for applications development. It makes it possible to communicate with the database by means of screen forms. All simple data manipulation operations, such as selection, insertion, deletion and modification, are possible without any prior knowledge of SQL. More advanced operations are expressed in SQL.

The design and use of these forms is made convenient by the interactive environment of SQL*Forms in which application prototypes can be quickly and easily developed. Like the database, the screen forms can be added to and altered.

During the design of a screen form, it is possible to define a wide variety of actions on each field. These can include introducing data, controlling returned data and end-user help (choosing from a list of values, messages, etc).

If new lines are to be inserted into a table of a given database using SQL, the person who carries out this task must first of all know SQL. Then, he must repeat the same operation for each line that is to be entered, changing the values on each occasion.

The risk of errors both at the syntax and at the data levels increases the more this operation is repeated. Of course, use of the SQL*Plus editor can greatly reduce the chances of errors, but it cannot entirely eliminate them.

If, however, a screen form already designed by SQL*Forms is used, not only is one freed from the syntactical constraints of SQL but the data to be entered into the database is automatically 'filtered'. On entering a given field, the user can obtain assistance from a list of the possible values for this field. Another important advantage of SQL*Forms is the facility of 'triggers' that initiate one or more actions before or after a given operation. They are of particular value in maintaining referential integrity between two tables, by deleting or inserting lines in a table when a second table is updated. If a product is deleted, this will automatically trigger the deletion of all commands relating to this product, an action that remains transparent to the user.

This chapter is devoted to a general presentation of SQL*Forms. We begin by describing the different steps to be followed for creating, generating and executing a form, together with a description of the architecture of SQL*Forms. We then introduce the terminology used. Subsequent sections outline the processes of form creation, modification and execution. Triggers are discussed at the end.

11.2 SQL*Forms

11.2.1 Design and use of forms

SQL*Forms may be considered from two different points of view:

- designer
  SQL*Forms allows forms to be created, modified and deleted. Such use assumes a knowledge of the tool as well as the basic elements of SQL.

- user
  SQL*Forms is a tool for executing forms. It allows the database to be queried and updated. Because the forms are already created, the system is much easier to use and does not require a knowledge of SQL. An added advantage is the use of function keys to replace conventional SQL commands.

Successful achievement of an SQL*Forms application requires the completion of three successive and independent phases: design, compilation and execution.

Phase 1 : design
This phase consists of designing the forms by defining the actions to be carried out on the data, the tables and columns involved and the appearance of the form, that is, the arrangement of the data in the form. The designer can either use the default options or insert values that best suit his needs. The design is built by moving through a tree-structured sequence of windows. Choosing an action normally either causes a new window to be opened superimposed over the previous ones, or takes the designer back to the preceding window. The result of this stage is a file containing the description of the form. The file name is the same as that of the form but with the extension INP.

Phase 2 : compilation
The result of the design phase is a non-executable 'source' file. The compilation phase consists first of an analysis of this file; then, if there are

no errors, it generates an executable file with the same name as the source file but with the extension FRM. If there are any errors, one must return to phase 1 and correct them.

Phase 3 : execution
This phase consists of dry running the application. Here the form is executed with a test run including all possible operations. Any anomalies found may be corrected in the source file by going back to phase 1. If there are no errors, the form can be put into actual use.

11.2.2 Architecture of SQL*Forms
Each of the phases described in the previous section has an SQL*Forms module allocated to it. These modules are: SQLFORMS, IAG and RUNFORM (see figure 11.1).

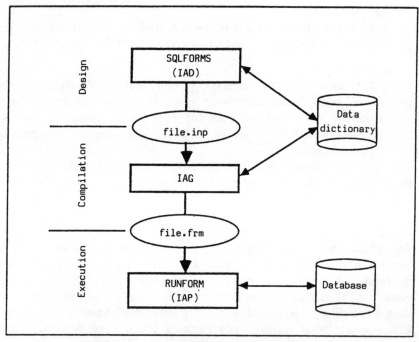

*Figure 11.1 Functioning of SQL*Forms*

Note in figure 11.1 the use of the data dictionary when designing and compiling a form. SQL*Forms uses the data dictionary to assist the designer by giving him information such as the list of accessible tables and the names of the columns in each table. The dictionary is used during compilation as well to cross check that the data provided during the design phase conforms with that in the database. Finally, when a form is generated, it is stored in the dictionary.

The SQLFORMS module, also called IAD (Interactive Application Designer), is responsible for the creation and modification of forms. It is activated by means of the following command:

```
SQLFORMS [options] [form_name] [user/pass_word]
```

The options determine some aspects of the display and possible redirection of inputs and outputs (see Oracle manuals for a list of these options). The form name may correspond to that of the form to be modified. If this form does not exist, it will be created. The user name and password are mandatory for the execution of SQLFORMS. If they are not given here, SQLFORMS begins with a window that asks for them.

The IAG module (Interactive Application Generator) generates executable forms. It receives an INP file as input, compiles it and generates a type FRM executable file. The syntax for initiating this module is:

```
IAG source_file [options]
```

The source file must correspond to an existing file called 'source_file.INP'.

Finally, the RUNFORM module, also called IAP (Interactive Application Processor), is the one that executes the FRM files. To activate it, the following command is entered:

```
RUNFORM [options] form_name [user/pass_word]
```

As with the SQLFORMS module, the user name and password will be required before the form can be executed if they are not provided in the RUNFORM command.

11.2.3 Terminology used in SQL*Forms

Throughout this chapter we shall use the following terminology:

FORM : A mixture of text and fields that permit the easy insertion, updating and selection of data in the database. A form may consist of one or more screen pages.

SCREEN PAGE : That part of the form that is visible on a screen page.

BLOCK : A subset of data in a form that relates to a specific table. A block may not contain fields that belong to more than one table. A form may be mono-block or multi-block.

RECORD : A line that comes from the database.

FIELD : The basic element of a block that can be used for the display, input or modification of data. A field is often shown in inverse video or underlined.

TRIGGER : A set of SQL*Forms and/or SQL commands that are executed when an event occurs.

11.2.4 Function keys and SQL*Forms

One of the features that enhance and facilitate the use of SQL*Forms is the provision of control via function keys. Most operations during the design and execution phases are carried out with these keys.

The roles of the function keys depend on the configuration chosen at installation of SQL*Forms. For this reason we shall not refer to actual keys such as F1, F2, etc, but we will use descriptive names in square brackets, such as [Accept], [Quit], etc. It is left to the reader to relate these to the function keys of his own system.

The roles of the function keys also change depending on whether one is in the design phase (SQLFORMS) or the execution phase (RUNFORM). In what follows we will describe the roles of the function keys in both contexts. The meaning of any key can be obtained at any time during the design and execution phases.

Roles of function keys during design phase
During the design of a form the keys are used principally to control the appearance of the form. The following list gives the main function key roles; those marked with (*) have a similar role in the execution of a form:

[Right](*)	shift cursor right
[Left](*)	shift cursor left
[Up]	shift cursor to line above
[Down]	shift cursor to line below
[Next Field](*)	move to next field
[Previous Field](*)	move to previous field
[Insert/Replace](*)	switch to replace mode or to insert mode
[Delete Char](*)	delete characters
[Clear Field](*)	fill a field with blanks
[Create Field]	create a field
[Select]	make a choice from a menu
[Select Block]	select a block
[Define]	define characteristics of a field or block
[Cut]	cut part from a block and place in a buffer
[Paste]	paste the contents of a buffer
[Draw Box/Line]	draw a box or a line
[Undo]	cancel the last instruction
[Accept]	confirm a choice
[Quit](*)	leave the current stage
[Print](*)	display a screen page
[Function Keys](*)	display the role of each function key.

Role of function keys during execution
During execution the function keys operate chiefly on data. At this level the appearance of the form cannot be altered. We give the main function keys and their roles below. Those that have the same function as that during design are omitted from this list (they are to be found in the previous list marked (*)):

[Duplicate Field]	assigns to the field indicated the contents of the same field of the preceding record
[Duplicate Record]	duplicates the contents of the preceding record in the current record
[Enter Query]	place SQL*Forms in wait state for data from the fields that will serve as selection criteria
[Execute Query]	execute a query
[Commit]	verify transaction
[Next Primary Key]	move to field considered to be next primary key
[Next Record]	move to the next record
[Next Record Set]	next set of records
[Next Block]	move to next block
[Previous Block]	move to previous block
[Help]	display a help message
[List of Values]	display the list of possible values for the current field
[Display Error]	display the last error found
[Menu Block]	display the block containing the menu of blocks accessible in this form
[Clear Record]	fill current record with blanks
[Clear Block]	fill all block records with blanks
[Clear Form]	fill the whole form with blanks
[Delete Record]	delete the current record.

11.3 Process for creating a form

Creating a form with SQL*Forms involves traversing a tree structure of windows and a choice of actions. A window is formed by a set of verbs that define the actions that may be carried out on the objects in SQL*Forms. Creating a form breaks down into the following process:

a) name a form
b) for each block in the form
  b1) create the block
  b2) for each field in the block
    b2.1)   place the field in the block
    b2.2)   fix or modify the field label
    b2.3)   define the properties of the field
  b3) improve the appearance of the block (underline, box, etc)
  b4) define the properties of the block
c) save the form
d) generate the corresponding form.

There are two ways of creating a form. The first is the default type of form using the the simple definition provided in SQL*Forms. This uses the field labels found in the database; these are arranged in a standard way by SQL*Forms according to their number and their length.

The second method is to use an editor to create a personalised form.

To gain a rapid understanding of SQL*Forms, we will illustrate the first method by creating a form called CLIENTFORM, by means of which we can manipulate data in the Client table. To do this, we will use the default approach. We will create default blocks, based on labels and a standard display provided by SQL*Forms, which we may change later.

The concept of default application in SQL*Forms allows the main functions of the application to be quickly created and tested, thus facilitating prototyping.

11.3.1 Naming and creating the form

Once SQL*Forms has begun, a first window CHOOSE FORM appears (see figure 11.2). It contains a space for the name to be inserted.

```
┌─────────────────────────────────────────┐
│              CHOOSE FORM                 │
│     Name                                 │
│                                          │
│     ----------------------------         │
│     Actions:                             │
│     CREATE        MODIFY        LIST      │
│     RUN           DEFINE        LOAD      │
│     FILE          GENERATE                │
└─────────────────────────────────────────┘
```

Figure 11.2 The CHOOSE FORM window

Apart from the space for the name the CHOOSE FORM window contains the following verbs:

- CREATE create a new form
- MODIFY modify an existing form
- LIST list all forms contained in the data dictionary
- RUN execute a form
- DEFINE define the attributes of the form
- LOAD load a form developed on another version or installation of SQL*Forms
- FILE save, cancel or make a copy of a form
- GENERATE generate an executable file from the form.

After the name of the form has been specified (CLIENTFORM), selection of the CREATE verb activates the CHOOSE BLOCK window for blocks to be manipulated (see figure 11.3).

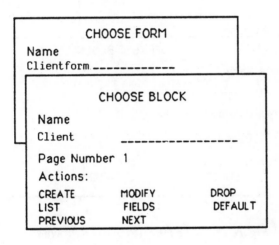

Figure 11.3 The CHOOSE BLOCK window

The CHOOSE BLOCK window contains a Name field for the block name to be specified, the page number in the block and the following verbs:

- CREATE create a block
- MODIFY modify a block
- DROP delete a block
- LIST list all blocks
- FIELDS display the list of the fields
- DEFAULT create a default block
- PREVIOUS access the previous block
- NEXT access the following block.

Selecting the DEFAULT option displays the DEFAULT BLOCK window (figure 11.4) which contains the name of the table on which the block will be defined, the number of lines to be displayed, the position of the first line in the block and two actions to list the database tables (TABLES) and the columns of a specific table.

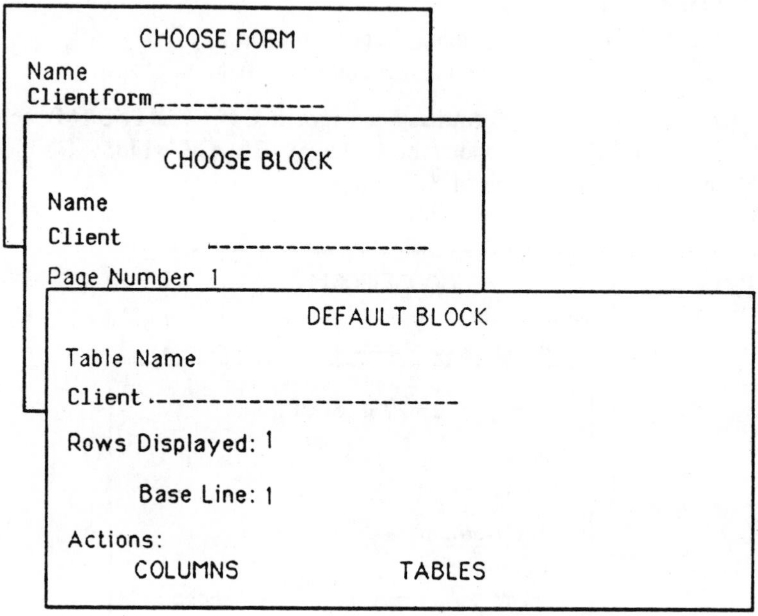

```
CHOOSE FORM
Name
Clientform_____


        CHOOSE BLOCK
  Name
  Client      _____
  Page Number  1

                DEFAULT BLOCK
   Table Name
   Client .----------------------
   Rows Displayed: 1

       Base Line: 1

   Actions:
        COLUMNS              TABLES
```

Figure 11.4 The DEFAULT BLOCK window

Selection of the action TABLES displays the database tables (Client, Order, Product and Sale). As we wish to manipulate the data in the Client table, we select it from the TABLE LIST window. This operation is not necessary if we know the table required and exactly what it is called.

The name Client is placed in the Table Name zone of the DEFAULT BLOCK. Selection of the action COLUMNS then displays the list of columns in the Client table. One can specify all columns or only a part to appear in the corresponding block. For example, we will choose all columns except specterm.

To see what the contents of the form will be, we move back to the CHOOSE BLOCK window and alter the Client block by choosing the MODIFY action. We then obtain the default form shown in figure 11.5.

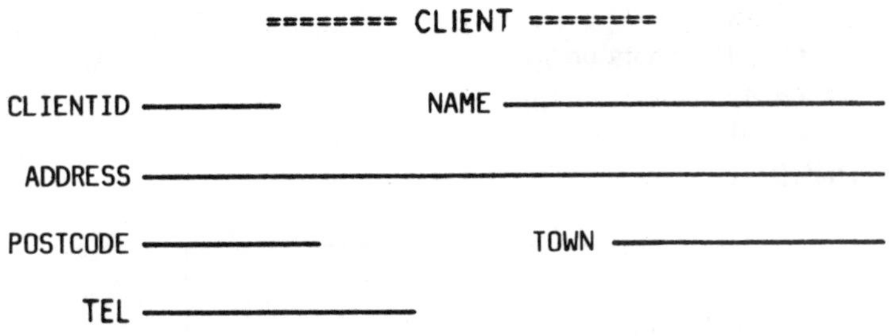

```
======== CLIENT ========
```

CLIENTID ————————   NAME ————————————————————

ADDRESS ————————————————————————————————————

POSTCODE ———————————   TOWN ————————————

TEL ———————————————

Figure 11.5 The default form

11.3.2 Altering the default block

We can now alter the presentation of this block by making the column names more meaningful. The title can be changed to CLIENT HANDLING and CLIENTID to NUMBER. We can also put a frame around the block. It should be noted that modifying the form can also extend to the screen position and properties of the fields. We then get the form shown in figure 11.6.

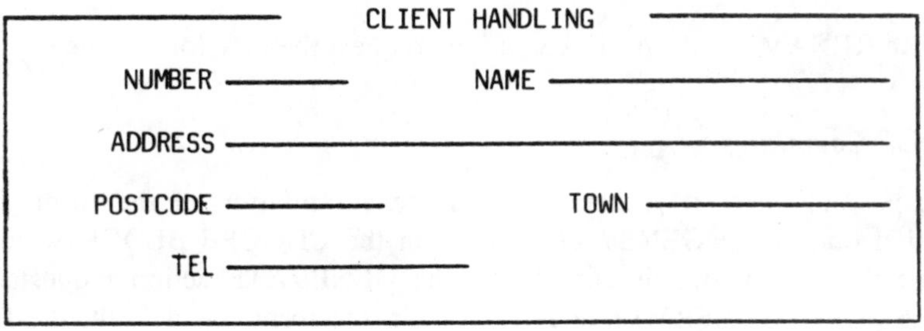

```
┌────────────────── CLIENT HANDLING ──────────────────┐
│      NUMBER ————————          NAME ———————————————   │
│     ADDRESS —————————————————————————————————————    │
│    POSTCODE ———————————        TOWN ————————————     │
│         TEL ———————————————                          │
└──────────────────────────────────────────────────────┘
```

Figure 11.6 The modified form

11.3.3 Saving the form

Now that the Client form is created, it must be saved, so that it can be restored later. This is done by means of the FILE action in the CHOOSE FORM window. The FILE window (figure 11.7) offers the following actions:

- SAVE   save
- DISCARD   abandon
- SAVE AS   make a copy
- RENAME   rename
- DROP   destroy.

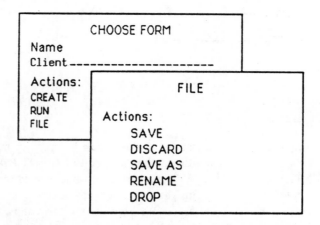

Figure 11.7 The FILE window

The RENAME and SAVE AS actions request the new form name.

11.3.4 Compiling

The second phase of construction is the compilation of the form. It is carried out by the GENERATE action in the CHOOSE BLOCK window. Once the compilation is completed, the GENERATE action requests the name of the file (.FRM) that is to contain the form. By default, the form name is suggested.

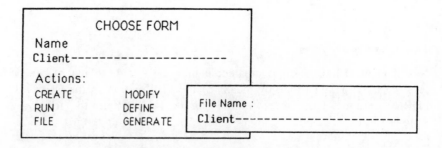

Figure 11.8 Generating a form

We now come out of SQL*Forms and execute the IAG processor in the following way:

```
IAG -to Client
```

The IAG generation process takes as source the client.inp file and produces a client.frm file.

11.3.5 Case of a multi-block form

A form may comprise more than one block. In the example shown in figure 11.9, there are two blocks, one for clients and the other for orders. The first block is a mono-record: only one record is displayed at a time. The second block is multi-record: four records are displayed at the same time. They are the orders from the same client. For this reason the client number does not appear in the second block.

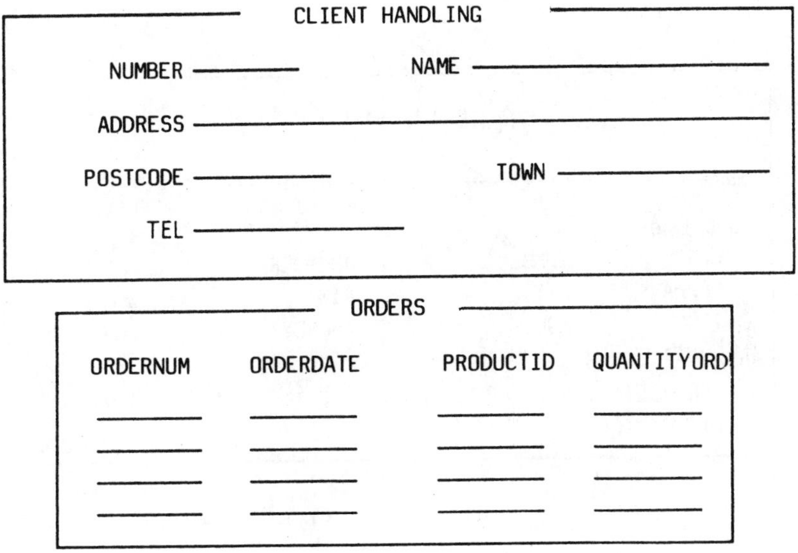

Figure 11.9 A multi-block form

11.4 Altering a form

The ability to alter an existing form allows new functions to be taken into account and permits the application to be adapted to new needs. Such alteration may involve the addition of new blocks, or altering or deleting blocks that already belong to this form.

11.4.1 Adding and altering blocks

We have already seen the particular case of creating a block by default. Alternatively, a block editor called the screen painter can be used to create a new block (or modify an existing one). This can be used to add, define, change or delete the labels in the block. Like a graphics editor, it offers graphics (line tracing, cut/paste), and textual functions (text creation, deletion and editing) for moving objects and creating others.

The DEFINE FIELD window (see figure 11.10) allows the properties of a field to be defined. This window is made up of the following information:

- sequence number of the attribute in the block
- the field name
- the type of field
- the actions TRIGGER, ATTRIBUTES, VALIDATION, COMMENT and COLUMNS.

```
┌─────────────────────────────────────────────────────────────┐
│                     DEFINE FIELD          Seq # 1            │
│                                                               │
│   Name    ──────────────────────────────────────────         │
│  Data Type:                                                   │
│     CHAR        NUMBER        RNUMBER        DATE             │
│     ALPHA       INT           RINT          JDATE            │
│     TIME        MONEY         RMONEY        EDATE            │
│  Actions:                                                     │
│     TRIGGER        ATTRIBUTES        VALIDATION              │
│     COMMENT        COLUMNS                                   │
└─────────────────────────────────────────────────────────────┘
```

Figure 11.10 The DEFINE FIELD window

The action ATTRIBUTES displays the window SPECIFY ATTRIBUTES (figure 11.11) which allows the following to be specified:

- the column in a database table which corresponds to this field (Database Field)
- the field is a key (Primary Key); in this case the need to ensure uniqueness control must be specified in SPECIFY BLOCK OPTIONS
- whether the contents will be hidden or not
- whether a new value may be input (Input allowed)
- whether the field may be used in a select condition (Query allowed)

- whether the value is modifiable if the value is NULL
- whether the length is fixed
- whether the value is mandatory
- whether the value appears automatically in capitals
- whether the system skips to the next field automatically
- whether a help screen is provided automatically
- whether there is echo or not.

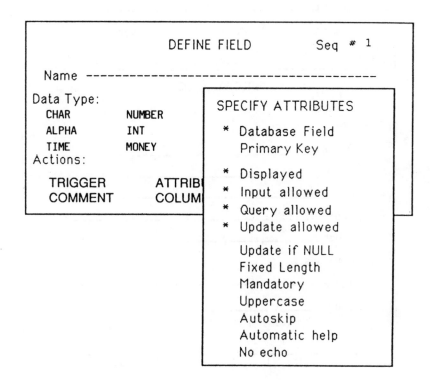

Figure 11.11 The SPECIFY ATTRIBUTES window

The VALIDATION action displays the SPECIFY VALIDATION window (figure 11.12) which allows the following properties to be specified:

- maximum field length
- maximum length when the field is used in a query condition
- the block and original field if the value of the field to be created is to be copied from another block
- default value, which may be a system value ($$DATE$$,$$TIME$$) or one from another field

- minimum and maximum values; these values are used by SQL*Forms to prevent the user from inputting a value outside the fixed interval
- the column and the table that can hold valid values for this field; at the moment of capture the user can list these values to select from
- a help screen that is displayed when the form is executed.

```
┌────────────────────────────────────────────────────────────┐
│                    DEFINE FIELD          Seq # 1            │
│     Name       --------------------------------------       │
│   ┌─────────────────────────────────────────────────────────┐
│   │                 SPECIFY VALIDATION                       │
│   │  Field Length ___              Query Length ___          │
│   │  Copy Field Value from:                                  │
│   │       Block _____  │
│   │       Field _____  │
│   │  Default    _____  │
│   │  Range Low  _____  │
│   │       High  _____  │
│   │  List of Values:                                         │
│   │       Table _____  │
│   │       Column _____  │
│   │  Help:                                                   │
│   │             _____  │
│   └─────────────────────────────────────────────────────────┘
└────────────────────────────────────────────────────────────┘
```

Figure 11.12 The SPECIFY VALIDATION window

The COMMENT action permits some textual comment to be added to the attribute.

The COLUMNS action fixes the column that corresponds to the field to be created.

11.4.2 Deleting a block

To delete a block from a form, the CHOOSE BLOCK window must be activated. Then, the name of the block to be deleted is provided and the

DROP verb is selected. This action only deletes the fields from the form; any text relating to this block remains. To delete that as well, the form editor must be used.

11.5 Executing a form

11.5.1 Introduction

To execute a form, the module RUNFORM must be activated as described in section 11.2.2. This causes the first page of the form to appear. All the operations established during the design phase can then be executed by using the function keys. We will see in the following sections how to input data into the database, and how to modify and delete data. As an illustration, we will use the form defined in section 11.3.2.

11.5.2 Inputting data into the database

At the start, the cursor is positioned automatically on the first field of the first block on the first page, and all the fields are initialised with blanks. We can now begin to input data. When the cursor is located on a field, a message is displayed in the message line as a guide to the user. Often it contains the prompt to use the [List of Values] key to obtain the list of values valid for this field. The sequence is as follows:

1) Strike [List of Values]; the first value in the list is displayed.
2) Strike [Next Field] to see the next value in the list.
3) Strike [Quit] if the value seen is the one required, or [Next Field] to continue through the list.

When a value has been input into a field, strike [Next Field] to move on to the next field. Most fields have a controlled input value. By striking [Next Field], there is the danger of getting an error message. We must then correct [Next Field] and strike it again. It is not mandatory to input values into all fields. Incomplete data may be added later. We can therefore return to a field to correct it before it is recorded by keying [Next Field] a number of times.

Once all the fields have been traversed, we have a choice between:

1) Verifying what we have input by keying [Commit]; in this case the block is automatically set to blanks, and we can input other values.
2) Strike [Next Record]; in this case, all that we have just input is stored in a buffer (work zone) and we can input other records. So long as we have not verified by keying [Commit], we can return to the previous records and correct them.

The keys [Duplicate Field] and [Duplicate Record] are useful when the value of a field or of all the fields of the current record is identical to that of the preceding record.

If a form contains more than one block, we use the [Next Block] and [Previous Block] keys to move from one block to another. We do not have to validate before moving from one block to another.

11.5.3 Selecting data

To consult the database, there are two approaches:

1) Traverse the data sequentially.
2) Select specific records according to given criteria.

Sequential traversal
Here it is a question of accessing all the lines in a table. To do this, one has to choose the appropriate block and then strike the [Execute Query] key. The data is then selected and stored in a buffer and the first record is displayed. The key [Next Record] and [Previous Record] allows the records to be scrolled in both directions. Messages are displayed to indicate the start or the end of a list.

Select specific records
The user here wishes to select a subset of data that satisfies particular criteria (for example all the customers in the town of Bournemouth). These criteria may concern one or more fields in the block. To make this selection, the procedure is:

1) Strike [Enter Query].
2) Input into the appropriate fields the comparison values using [Next Field] to move from field to field.
3) Strike [Execute Query] to execute the query.

The data that satisfies the selection criteria is then selected and stored in a buffer and the first record is displayed. As before, the [Next Record] and [Previous Record] keys may be used to scroll the records in both directions.

When the selection criteria includes an inequality ($<$, $<=$, $>$ or $>=$), the comparison constant must be prefixed with the corresponding sign. For more complex comparisons, such as those that use the BETWEEN, LIKE, IN, NOT, AND and OR operators, it becomes necessary to use variables. A variable is any identifier (the & symbol followed by a string of characters that is input into the field used to make the selection). When we execute the query ([Execute Query]), the message 'Query Where...?' appears in the status line. We reply by keying the condition to be satisfied by the variable;

for example, '&A IN (1,2,3)'. The syntax to be followed is the same as for the WHERE clause in SQL. This is the only instance where some prior knowledge of SQL is required of the form user.

11.5.4 Modifying data

To modify data, it first has to be selected by one of the methods described in the previous section. One then needs to position oneself on the record to be altered and make the change. We can then verify the modification immediately after each record or at the end. The same remarks concerning use of the [List of Values] key are valid during modifications.

11.5.5 Deleting data

Again, to delete a record, it has first to be selected. The cursor is then placed on one of the fields of the record to be deleted. Activating the [Delete Record] key completes the deletion of the record. This deletion is only effective in the database when the operation is verified with [Commit]. So long as a deletion has not been verified, it may still be cancelled by [Quit].

11.6 Triggers

11.6.1 Introduction

A trigger is a sequence of actions to be executed when a particular event occurs.

A trigger is said to be at form, block or field level, depending on whether the event to which it is assigned concerns a form, block or field. Triggers may be executed at the following times:

- entry : at entry or when the cursor is located in a new block or field
- query : after the records have been found in the database
- modification : after a value has been modified, or before/after verification of an insertion, an update or a deletion of a record from the database
- exit : at the moment of leaving the form, or when the cursor leaves a block, a record or a field.

A trigger may also be defined to assign actions to function keys, or to define a set of external actions (at user level) that will be recalled when another trigger is executed.

11.6.2 Types of trigger

Triggers may serve to:

- carry out controls at the level of block fields
- transfer data from the current block to other blocks.

There are eight types of trigger at block level. They can correspond to queries, validations, records or navigation between blocks:

query triggers

pre-query : a pre-query trigger is executed before execution of the query. The trigger commands may access data supplied by the user, but not that coming from the database.

post-query : a post-query trigger is executed once for each record that makes up the result and just before the latter is brought from the database and displayed on the screen for the first time. The trigger commands may access all values of the record found.

The pre-query and post-query triggers are executed with the [Execute Query] key.

commit triggers

pre-delete : executed once for each record deleted just before the record is actually deleted from the database. The trigger commands may access all data in the record and in the line.

post-delete : executed once for each record deleted after the record has actually been deleted from the database. Commands may not access values in the line.

pre-insert : executed once for each record, just before the line is actually inserted into the database. Commands may access all data in the line and in the record.

post-insert : executed once for each record, just after the record has been inserted into the table. Commands may access all data in the line and in the record.

pre-update : executed once for each record, just before the update is effected in the database. Commands may access all values of the record that have just been modified and those of the column that is not yet modified.

post-update : executed once for each record updated, just after the corresponding line has been modified in the table. Commands may access all values of the updated line in the table and those of the record.

Use of block level triggers varies according to type:

- Pre-query triggers may be used to restrict access to the table to particular periods of the day and to certain types of query.
- Post-query triggers may be used to carry out statistical calculations after the data has been found.
- Pre-insert, pre-delete and pre-update triggers serve to validate data: existence of the value to be input in another table, coherence with a value located in another zone, etc.
- Post-insert, post-update and post-delete triggers may be used to strengthen the coherence and updating of data relating to that just input.
- Trigger : function key

A trigger may be used to redefine the function of any key. This type of trigger may be defined at the field, block or form level. The range of the trigger is the field, block or form at the level at which it is defined.

If there is more than one trigger of the same type defined, the higher level one takes precedence.

Some function keys may not be redefined. Those that may be redefined appear in the Oracle installation guide and the user manual.

- Trigger : user

These types of trigger are executed by other triggers and not after events.

11.6.3 Internal functioning of a trigger

As we have already seen, a trigger is a set of commands that are executed when an event occurs.

Each command represents a step in the trigger and it can be one of the following:

- an SQL command to fetch and/or modify data in a table or in a field
- an SQL*Forms command, as is the case with commands assigned to function keys
- user modules (User Exit) written in high level langauges, or Oracle service commands.

The steps of a trigger are executed in sequence one after another. The execution of a step is conditioned by the end of the step that precedes it.

The end of a step may result in one of the following states:

- success : the command is executed and execution of the next command starts. If it was the last command, the trigger has executed successfully
- failure : the command is cancelled and as a result the trigger is halted
- fatal error : SQL*Forms has exceeded memory capacity.

The modifications carried out in steps are visible to the next step. The success or failure of a step depends on the nature of the command. For example, the success of a SELECT, UPDATE or DELETE command is demonstrated by at least one line inserted, updated or deleted in the table. If no line has been affected, the step fails.

The success or failure of an external module (User Exit) depends on the internal logic of the latter. The trigger type conditions the subsequent actions. In fact:

- the success of a pre- and post-insert, update and delete trigger causes changes in the database. Failure stops the validations and causes those already made to be cancelled
- the success of a pre-query trigger allows the query to continue; if it fails, the query stops
- the success of a post-query trigger leaves the fetched data in the workspace; its failure replaces it with blanks.

12 Integrated Spreadsheet SQL*Calc

12.1 Introduction

When Oracle Corporation became interested in the microcomputer market, it had to adapt to this market and to its customers habits; and this market was remarkable for its addiction to spreadsheets.

Spreadsheets were the first packages to have an impact in the field of microcomputer software. Their ease of use and adaptability to a wide range of applications have ensured their widespread use. The first in the field was Visicalc, joined a few years later by others among which the best known today are Multiplan and Lotus 1-2-3.

Oracle's adaptation to this environment was marked by the introduction to its range of an additional tool to fulfil the traditional role of a spreadsheet and allowing the data controlled by the DBMS to be manipulated as well. This is SQL*Calc.

SQL*Calc is therefore a tool integrated with the Oracle DBMS and is compatible with Lotus 1-2-3. As its name suggests, its functions combine those of SQL and of a spreadsheet. SQL*Calc-type access facilities can also be incorporated into Lotus 1-2-3.

The main functions of spreadsheets are:

- Presentation of data in tabular form (already a feature in common with relational databases).
- Dialogue via menus for the description and manipulation of data.
- Use of formulas to express links between data.
- Automatic recalculation after modification of data.

Among the additional functions offered by SQL*Calc compared with other spreadsheets like Lotus 1-2-3 we can mention:

- The use of data controlled by Oracle in the worksheet in the same way as other data.
- The updating of Oracle data through manipulations on the worksheet.
- The creation of tables in the database whose structure and data derive from the worksheet.

To these may be added the other features of the Oracle DBMS, such as security, confidentiality and data sharing.

109

Furthermore, SQL*Calc is not confined to the PC environment; it is available on a wide variety of machines and systems.

In the following section we will describe the different ways of connecting with SQL*Calc, the structure of the worksheet and the roles of the function keys. Section 12.3 will discuss the main operations in a worksheet. Finally, section 12.4 will examine in more detail the use of SQL in worksheets.

12.2 Introduction to SQL*Calc

12.2.1 Connection

Connecting to SQL*Calc may be done in two ways depending on the manipulations to be carried out:

- use SQL*Calc just like a spreadsheet without calling upon the additional features offered by Oracle
- use SQL*Calc like a spreadsheet and an interface for manipulating Oracle data.

In the first case, the Oracle kernel does not need to be active and it is not necessary to have an account (a user name and a password) to run SQL*Calc. Start-up of SQL*Calc is then made with the SQLCALC command. A first screen appears for a few moments, then a second. The latter requests an identification name. A carriage return then reveals the worksheet.

In the second case, one first needs to establish that Oracle is already active, or if not activate it. Then, connection to SQL*Calc with a given Oracle user name may be made in two ways:

```
SQLCALC user_name/password
```

or

```
SQLCALC
```

The name and/or password will be requested by Oracle if they are not specified.

It should be noted that even when SQL*Calc is run only as a spreadsheet, it is possible to connect with an Oracle user name at any time by means of the LOGON command. This command also allows the database tables to be changed without leaving the worksheet. In this way one can work in the same worksheet on data belonging to several users, although from the practical point of view such possibilities are rare because of the need for data to be held securely.

When SQL*Calc is active, we can begin our work. A blank worksheet first appears. If we want to work on an existing sheet, we need to load it with the RETRIEVE command selected from the FILE menu (see 12.3.5).

Note that each worksheet is stored in a file with the default extension CAL. There is no need to provide the extension when referring to this file. The user can also choose another extension; in this case he must always specify it to designate the file.

The Quit command allows one to exit from the SQL*Calc spreadsheet.

12.2.2 Structure of a worksheet

The dialogue between SQL*Calc and the user is carried out on a screen page consisting of the worksheet and a dialogue area (figure 12.1). The sheet has the same structure as that of Lotus 1-2-3, with a few differences. Users familiar with the Lotus screen will easily adapt.

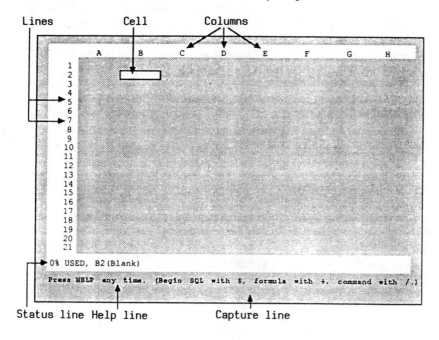

Figure 12.1 Structure of a worksheet

The worksheet is made up of a set of cells. A cell is the basic element that can contain a numeric value, text, a formula or an SQL command. Each cell is referenced by its coordinates: a letter going from A to IV for the columns and a line number going from 1 to 8192. The first cell is therefore A1 (or a1) and the last is IV8192 (or iv8192). A set of adjacent cells constitutes a zone designated by its first and last cells separated by a point (A1.A20 for the first 20 cells in column A, and C10.E15 for the cells of lines 10 to 15 in columns C, D and E). These coordinates are called absolute coordinates. It is also possible to designate a cell by relative coordinates. In this case, lowercase letters must be used. This distinction is very important when copying cells containing formulas or SQL commands. The inverse option may also be selected (lowercase for absolutes and uppercase for relatives). A name can also be given to a zone (see NAME command in 12.3.2).

The visible part of the sheet on the screen is called the window. The user can work simultaneously on two windows by dividing the screen into two parts. How it is divided (vertically or horizontally) and the relative proportions of the parts may be chosen by the user.

The dialogue zone consists of a status line, a help line and a data input line.

The status line is the one that appears at the foot of the screen just under the worksheet. It is used by SQL*Calc to display data and messages in case of incorrect manoeuvres. At the start of this line SQL*Calc always displays the percentage of available memory that is being used by SQL*Calc for storing data. Then, depending on the circumstances, one of the following items of information appears:

- the version number of SQL*Calc when connection has just been made
- the features of the cell pointed to: the address of the cell, the type of data contained (blank, number, text, formula or SQL command) and finally the contents, if any
- a possible error message after execution of an SQL command or the evaluation of a formula.

The contents of the last two lines of the screen vary depending on whether one is in input or in command mode. The input mode is the default mode. In this mode, the penultimate line is called the help line, and the following line is the one that serves as data input line for the cells. When a cell is pointed to, the data (including formulae and SQL commands) is first captured in this line. It is only copied into the corresponding cell after verification (Return key).

Transfer to the command mode is made by striking the '/' character. In this case, the penultimate line becomes the command line and the last line becomes the one for the description of each command. The command line appears like a menu consisting of a set of commands. The next line gives a summary description of the command pointed to and perhaps the set of its subcommands. More detailed help regarding the command may be obtained by striking the F1 key. Movement from one command to another is via the directional arrow keys. When a command has no subcommands, it is executed and one returns to the input mode. Return to this mode may also be achieved using the Escape key which interrupts the command mode.

12.2.3 Function keys

The most frequent operations in SQL*Calc can be accessed by the function keys. As in SQL*Forms, the role of these keys may vary from one installation to another. It is for this reason that in what follows we will designate each key by the function it carries out (shown in square brackets). We will then give as an example the corresponding number on a PC keyboard (in parentheses).

[HELP] (F1): The help obtained varies depending on the place where this key is struck.

[EDIT] (F2): Copies the contents of the cell pointed to into the input zone for editing. The delete (Del) and insert (Ins) keys may be used in editing.

[NAME] (F3): Gives the list of files available containing worksheets (with .CAL extension).

[GOTO] (F5): Points to a given cell.

[WINDOW] (F6): Points to the last cell used in the other window when working in two windows. Has no effect when working on one window only.

[QUERY] (F7): Executes a query.

[TABLE] (F8): Gives the list of accessible tables.

[CALC] (F9): Recalculates the worksheet.

[COPIED] (F10): Executes an operation (formula or SQL command) copied from another cell.

In addition to the function keys, SQL*Calc uses the cursor control keys to move around the worksheet and the dialogue zone.

12.3 Main operations in a worksheet

In this section we will concern ourselves only with worksheet operations that do not call SQL. Those that do will be discussed in the next section.

The operations may be classified as follows:

- Operations applicable to any worksheet.
- Operations applicable to a zone.
- Operations for setting up.
- Insertion, deletion, movement and copying of lines and columns.
- Operations for manipulating files from the worksheet.

SQL*Calc uses tree-structured menus; the activation of a command selected from an initial menu may prompt the display of another menu containing options or subcommands. This may be repeated a few times before an executable command is reached.

To represent this hierarchy of commands, we adopt the following method:

```
/Command 1 Command 2...
```

where

- The '/' character represents the transfer to command mode.
- Command 1 is a command in the main menu.
- Command 2 is an option or a subcommand of Command 1, etc.

The selection of a command from a menu can be made by pointing to it with the cursor keys or by striking its initial letter. For example, the command Worksheet can be selected by keying W. The following line:

/W Options

means the subcommand Options from the Worksheet command chosen from the initial menu.

12.3.1 Operations applicable to any worksheet

The Worksheet command which is activated from the initial menu contains a set of subcommands that apply to the whole worksheet. They allow the following operations:

- Defining the options for the whole worksheet. The main options defined under /W Options are: automatic recalculation after every cell change, displaying or not the edges of the sheet and the mode for cell reference (uppercase – absolute and lowercase – relative, or the reverse).
- Clearing to blanks the complete worksheet. The contents are then lost after activation of the /W Erase command.
- Use of lines/columns as titles. The command /W Title defines titles for columns (/W Title Vertical), for lines (/W Title Horizontal) or for the two (/W Title Both). These titles will not move past when the other cells move past. The cells used as titles are no longer accessible. The command /W Title Clear cancels the titles and renders the cells used accessible again.
- Dividing the screen into two windows: it is possible with the /W Window command to separate the screen horizontally or vertically into two windows. This division is made in the line or column that follows that of the active cell. The two windows can be synchronised or not (/W Window Sync or Unsync); that is, moving the cursor in one window causes a similar displacement in the other window. The [Window] key is used to move from one window to the other. The command /W Window Clear returns to the single window mode.

12.3.2 Operations applicable to a zone

A zone is a set of adjacent cells. It is referenced by its first and last cells and it may have a name. The command /Range (shown as /R here) from the initial menu allows the following operations to be carried out on zones:

• *Definition of a zone*
The command /R Name allocates a name to a zone, deallocates it and provides a list of the names and references of the allocated zones.

• *Sorting a zone*
It is possible to sort the cells of a zone into increasing or decreasing order. The command is /R Sort. When the zone contains more than one column, one of these columns must be chosen as the sort key.

• *Protection of a zone*
To protect a zone from alteration, the /R Protect command must be used. When pointing to a cell that belongs to a protected zone, we see the letter P in the status line after the data type (for example, A10 (number,P) = 17). A message is displayed if we try to alter the contents of a protected cell. The cancel command is /R Unprotect.

• *Clearing a zone*
Just as the whole worksheet is cleared, a zone is cleared with the /R Erase command.

12.3.3 Set up operations

SQL*Calc is often used to produce spreadsheets that need to be well presented. The /Layout (/L) command allows the worksheet specification to be established (/L Worksheet), together with a line (/L Horiz-Row), a column (/L Column) or even a single cell (/L Field). It also allows predefined styles to be modified for later use (/L Modify-Styles).
   The possible formats are:

- Width : Alters the width of a column (only applies to the columns and to the whole worksheet).
- Style : Assigns one of the predefined styles to a cell, a column, a line or to the whole worksheet.
- Align : Justifies the contents to the right or to the left.
- Money : Shows numerical values rounded to two decimal places.
- Int : Rounds the contents to an integer (applies to numeric values).
- Exp : Represents numeric values in exponential form.
- Bar : Creates a bar chart made up of '=' signs placed next to one

another. The number of signs equals the value contained in the cell.
- General : Adopts the default presentation: text justified to the left, numbers justified to the right.
- Decimal : Fixes the number of decimal places.
- Reset : Cancels the set up.

12.3.4 Insertion, deletion and movement of lines and columns

SQL*Calc allows worksheets to be controlled dynamically. This is true not only for changing the contents of cells, but also for the overall structure of the worksheet. It is therefore possible to delete parts of the worksheet, insert others, and move lines or columns and copy one zone into another:

- Inserting lines or columns
  The /W Insert command inserts a certain number of lines or columns. The following lines or columns are shifted.
- Deleting lines or columns
  The /W Delete command deletes a set of lines or columns. The lines or columns are also shifted after the deletion.
- Moving a line or a column
  It is possible to move the current line or column into another part of the worksheet using the /W Move command. It is not possible to move several.
- Copy cells or zones
  The /Copy command copies from a cell or a zone into another cell or zone. All types of contents may be copied, including formulae and SQL commands. When a formula or an SQL command is copied, the relevant references are automatically adapted.

12.3.5 Manipulating files from a worksheet

SQL*Calc stores the worksheets on which it works in files. It therefore has several commands to manipulate these files:

• Loading worksheet into memory
When we connect with SQL*Calc, it begins by using a blank worksheet. If we want to work on another worksheet that has been stored previously, it has to be loaded with the command /F Retrieve (F for File). This command can be executed at any time but it is important to save the current file before doing so. Loading may affect the contents of the cells, the options and the formats or the complete worksheet.

• *Saving a worksheet*
The /F Save command is used to save the current worksheet.

• *Link with other worksheets*
It is possible to make a temporary or permanent link with another worksheet with the aim of extracting data from it. This link must be made via a named zone. The /F Link command is used for this. The command /F Link List will reveal a list of the links between the current worksheet and others. A permanent link may be removed with /F Link Delete.

• *Merging worksheets*
The command /F Merge is used to merge the current worksheet with another.

• *Printing a worksheet*
At any time the contents of the worksheet may be printed or output to a file. The /Print is used to print the whole worksheet, part of it (zone) or only what is visible on the screen. Print options may be selected (number of characters per line, top margin, bottom margin, etc).

• *Other utilities*
The /F Utilities command offers a choice of file manipulation commands, such as:

- list the files containing worksheets
- copy a file
- delete a file
- change directory.

12.4 Use of SQL in a worksheet

The user of SQL*Calc has two means of interacting with the database from the worksheet. The first is via SQL commands inserted in the cells in the same way as formulae, and the second is by using the Oracle menu in command mode. These two methods may be used simultaneously.

12.4.1 SQL command in cells

When the first character entered into a cell is '$', all the text that follows it is interpreted as an SQL command. This text may be any definition or data manipulation command. The syntax of these commands is sometimes slightly altered by the introduction of cell addresses. In what follows, a distinction is made between data selection commands and other types of command.

Data selection

Selection consists of copying a part of the database into a zone of the worksheet. This zone is called the target zone. Before beginning to key the selection command, the user must locate himself in the cell corresponding to the first line of the first column of the target zone. The syntax of the selection command has the following two additional features compared with that used in SQL:

- It is possible to use in the WHERE clause cell references from the worksheet to compare a column of a table with the contents of a cell. In this case, the cell reference is preceded by the '&'. For example, the expression 'name=&a3' means compare the values of the column 'name' in any table with the contents of cell a3 in the worksheet.
- An additional clause may be added to the selection command to identify the target zone. This is the INTO clause that follows the SELECT clause. It is of the form: 'INTO §start.end', where start and end are the references of the first and last cell in the target zone. If this clause is missing, SQL*Calc adds it automatically. The target zone taken by default is the one whose first cell contains the selection command and whose last depends on the size of the result.

Once entered, a query is first analysed syntactically. If it contains errors, a message indicating the type of error is displayed. If there are no errors, the query is evaluated to know the size of the result. The names of the columns selected are displayed first. If there is a match between the size of the result and that of the target zone, the result is then copied into the worksheet. If not, a message is displayed indicating that there has been positive or negative overflow of the target zone (that is, the size of the result is greater or less than that of the target zone). This message therefore contains the number of lines selected and requests the choice of an action from one of the following: insert all lines thereby displacing other lines in the worksheet, squash the overlapping lines, etc (see section 12.4.2 for the different possibilities). To avoid having to reply to these questions at each query, one option may be selected and fixed once and for all using the / Oracle Options command (see also 12.4.2). After the option is selected, the result is copied into the target zone.

Other SQL commands

All the other types of SQL command may be executed from the worksheet. The UPDATE command can update a table from data in the worksheet by introducing into the SET clause the reference of the cell containing the value to be substituted. For example, the command:

```
UPDATE Client SET name=§c12 WHERE name = 'Smith'
```

replaces the name 'Smith' in the Client table with the contents of cell c12.

It is also possible to insert data into a table in the database from data in the worksheet. For example, the command:

```
INSERT INTO Client (clientid, name) VALUES ($b2, $b3)
```

inserts respectively into the clientid and name columns of the Client table the values contained in cells b2 and b3.

Similarly, some lines can be deleted from a given table. The command:

```
DELETE FROM Client WHERE name=$c5
```

deletes all the lines from the Client table whose client name is the one contained in cell c5.

A cell may also contain an SQL data definition command such as the creation, alteration or deletion of a table. We will see in section 12.4.2 how to create a table whose structure and contents are copied from the worksheet.

12.4.2 Execution of SQL commands from the Oracle menu

To re-execute SQL commands that have already been entered into cells or to execute other Oracle commands, we need to move into the command mode (by striking '/') and activate the Oracle command in the main menu. This results in the display of another menu containing the following commands: Execute, Show-Info, Logon, Commit, Rollback, Options and Table.

Connecting to Oracle
Connection with Oracle is necessary to execute commands. The /Oracle command connects a user with Oracle at any time during an SQL*Calc session. When this command is activated, the system requests the user name and password. This command also allows one to change account during the same session.

Execution of SQL commands contained in the worksheet
When an SQL command is input into a cell, it is executed immediately. If it is a selection command, the data selected is copied into the worksheet. For an update command, the database is altered from the worksheet. In these two cases, the source data is liable to evolve in the course of an SQL*Calc session thus leading to some incoherence between the worksheet data and that contained in the database. To avoid this, SQL*Calc allows SQL commands to be re-executed at any time. It is thus possible to re-execute all, or only some, select, modify and delete commands.

Execution (or rather re-execution) of SQL commands is initiated by / Oracle Execute. Activation causes a menu to appear from which the type of operation to be executed may be specified: selection, modification, insertion, deletion or data protection.

/O Execute Select re-executes all or part of the selection commands from the worksheet. The contents of the worksheet are also altered by the results of queries that are executed.

/O Execute Update re-executes all or part of the modification commands for the database. The database is thus updated from the worksheet.

/O Execute Insert re-executes all or part of the data insertion commands into the database from the worksheet. The contents of the worksheet are not altered.

/O Execute Delete re-executes all or part of the commands for deleting data from the database. The database is thus updated, while the worksheet remains unaltered.

/O Execute Lock re-executes all or part of the commands for locking tables in the database.

Finally, /O Execute Copied executes all the cells marked '*COPIED*', that is, cells whose SQL queries have been copied from other cells. The function key [COPIED] (F10) has the same effect.

A selection command may have as result a set of values (set of lines and columns). The cardinality of this set is often unknown before execution of the query and it may therefore not match the size of the target zone. By default, this zone is the cell that contains the query. The size of the set of selected values may be either greater or less than that of the target zone. In the first case, we say that there is overflow and in the second, underflow.

Oracle has a command to handle this situation. It is the /O Options command which gives access to two subcommands: Overflow and Underflow.

a) case of overflow

The Overflow subcommand fixes the option to be taken. There are four to choose from:

- Automatic insertion of the results, shifting any following lines and columns as necessary. This is the Insert option.
- The lines and columns that extend beyond the target zone squash the following lines and columns. This is Overwrite.
- The lines and columns that extend beyond the zone are ignored. This is the Stop option.
- At the time of executing the query the user is asked to choose one of the above three options. This is the Ask option. It is the default if no option has been fixed.

b) case of underflow

The Underflow subcommand fixes the option to be taken. There are three to choose from:

- Deletion of the remaining lines and columns from the target zone. The following lines and columns are then shifted (forwards). This is the Delete option.
- Leave the unused cells empty. This is the Stop option.
- The Ask option is similar to the case with overflow.

Transaction management

When database update operations are initiated from the worksheet, all the alterations may be cancelled so long as they have not been committed explicitly or implicitly (by quitting SQL*Calc).

The /O Commit command verifies (confirms) alterations to the database made from the start of the session or since the last commit. After this command has been activated, it is no longer possible to cancel the modifications. The act of quitting SQL*Calc is an implicit verification.

The /O Rollback command cancels all modifications made to the database since the last commit or since the start of the session if no commit has been carried out.

Creating tables

One of the most important functions of SQL*Calc is the facility to create new tables in the database whose structure and contents are copied from the worksheet. The tabular structure of the worksheet is an aid to this operation, since each of its columns can have a name, a data type and a size.

The command that allows a table to be created in the database from the worksheet is /O Table. Once this command is activated, SQL*Calc asks for the references of the cells that will be used as the column names in the database. It then asks for the references of the cells from which the data to form the table will be copied.

Obtaining additional information

SQL*Calc has commands that can provide additional information about the available tables, SQL queries and the result of the last query executed. This information can be found from the /O Show-Info menu.

- The Error subcommand displays the last SQL command executed and the result of this execution (error).
- The SQL-Cells command gives a list of all the SQL commands in the worksheet.
- The My-Tables subcommand gives a list of all the user's tables.
- The All-Tables command gives a list of all tables accessible to the connected user.

13 Report and Menu Generators: SQL*Report and SQL*Menu

13.1 Report generator: SQL*Report

13.1.1 Introduction

SQL*Report is a report generator that can contain text and data that comes from the database. It produces a wide variety of documents in which part of the contents are variable. This variable part is the result of SQL selection commands. The documents generated may range from simple letters in which the name and address are extracted from the database to a complex report in tabular form that contains for example details about the orders for a given product.

There are two components to SQL*Report: the report generator (RPT) and the text formatter (RPF). The role of RPT is to select data from the database. The RPF uses this data to produce the document according to the format chosen by the user.

Figure 13.1 illustrates the different steps for producing a report.

The process for generating reports has as input a file called the control file. It contains:

- RPT commands to select data
- RPF commands to format data
- text that will appear in the report with the data selected from the database.

Execution of the RPT produces an intermediate file that contains:

- data selected from the database
- text input into the control file
- formatting commands.

Once obtained, the intermediate file is used by the RPF to format the selected data and the text provided by the user to produce expected report.

Recently, SQL*ReportWriter has been released. This replaces SQL*Report and provides additional facilities.

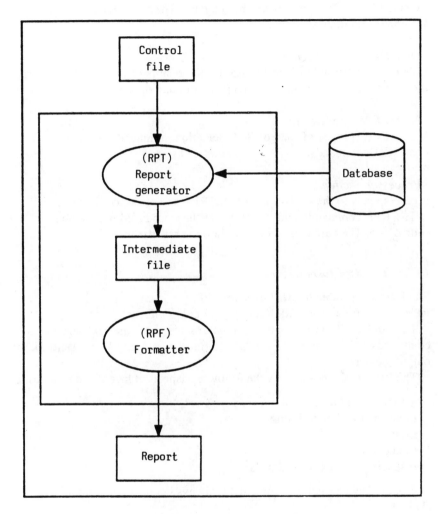

Figure 13.1 The steps for generating reports

13.1.2 Report generator (RPT)

The report generator is activated with the following command: RPT
source_file result_file [user/pass_word]

The source_file is the name of the control file and the result_file is the
name of the intermediate file generated by the RPT. If the user name and
the password are not provided with this command, they are requested.

The source_file is in fact a program, some commands of which will be executed by the RPT and others by the RPF. These commands are logically separated into three sections:

• *Data Declaration Section*
It defines the variables used for storing the results of the selection queries, the results of calculations (sum, average, etc) and the counters.

• *Macro Definition Section*
It defines two types of macro: SQL selection commands and macros made up of RPT commands.

• *Processor Section*
It corresponds to the execution of SQL, RPT and macro commands.
The RPF commands and the text may be introduced at any point in the source_file. They are copied directly into the result_file.

13.1.3 The RPF formatter

The following command will execute RPF:
RPF source_file [output_file][output_device][-switches]
The source_file is the one that contains the data, the text and the RPF commands. The result can be stored in the output_file or sent to the output_device.
The RPF commands specify the following aspects of layout and formatting:

- vertical and horizontal margins
- centring and underlining
- tabulation
- page numbering
- spacing and text insertion.

From the syntax point of view, RPF always begins with a point or the '#' character.
An important concept managed by the RPF is that of the 'table' or 'window'. A table (as distinct from the tables that make up the database), is a rectangular window described by its width, its height and the number of its columns. It may consist of a single column. A single character for example may be regarded as a single column table.
The DT command fixes the width of a table and assigns an identifier to it.

13.2 Menu-driven applications: SQL*Menu

13.2.1 Introduction

SQL*Menu is a tool that allows one to define and choose between several actions presented in the form of one or more menus. The actions generally refer to the execution of Oracle tool commands, such as SQL*Plus, SQL*Forms or SQL*Report or commands from the host system. It allows one to organise the execution of different actions in an application. The main advantages of organising an application in menu form are:

- a reduction in keying errors
- better security, since the number of executable commands is controlled
- a clearer picture of the application and the possibilities offered.

An application is normally presented in the form of tree-structured menus. The first is called the main menu. A choice made from the menu causes another menu to appear and so on until the executable commands are reached. One can also return to an earlier menu. Figure 13.2 illustrates such a structure.

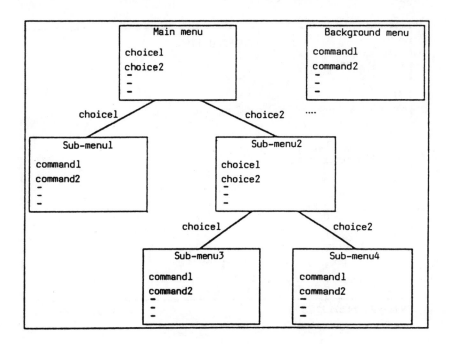

Figure 13.2 Menu tree structure

Note in figure 13.2 the menu called the background menu, referred to subsequently as BGM. It can be accessed from any other menu. It is optional and depends on the application. It normally contains the set of commands that are most often used in an application.

The visible part of a menu tree may vary from one user to another, since users are in fact classified. The menu choices vary from one class of users to another. The menu designer decides which classes of user may access the different options.

13.2.2 Layout of a menu

A menu consists of the following elements:

- a title (at the top and/or the bottom of the screen)
- a subtitle
- a list of options
- a choice line, and
- a line of general information, such as the date, the application name and the menu name.

Figure 13.3 shows an example of a menu for choosing either order entry or a further sub-menu for order reports.

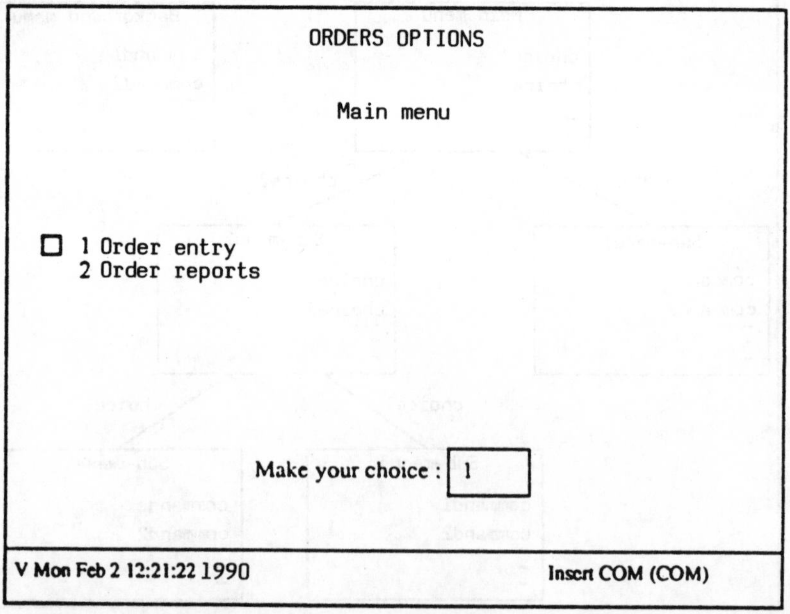

```
                         ORDERS OPTIONS

                           Main menu




    □  1 Order entry
       2 Order reports








                    Make your choice : │ 1           │


 V Mon Feb 2 12:21:22 1990                      Insert COM (COM)
```

Figure 13.3 A menu example

13.2.3 Using SQL*Menu

SQL*Menu makes use of some of the features of SQL*Forms, such as the function keys and the form type of presentation. This is why the installation of SQL*Forms is a prerequisite for the use of SQL*Menu.

SQL*Menu is activated by the command:

SQLMENU [application][user/pass_word][-option]

As in the other Oracle tools, if the user name and the password are not given, they will be requested before SQL*Menu starts.

The possible options are:

t type of terminal
l language used
q silent mode
v read data from a file
w write output to a file.

If an application name is given, the main menu of this application is displayed first. If no application is given, SQL*Menu displays a default menu, called APPLICATION MENU, that offers two options:

* develop new menus
* execute one of the existing applications.

Choosing the second option causes a second menu to appear that contains all accessible applications, while the first displays a menu containing these three options:

* create or modify an application
* generate the documentation for an application
* administration.

The third option only appears if the user has the DBA privilege.

The next three sections will be devoted to a discussion of each of these options.

13.2.4 Design and modification of an application

The design of an application based on menus involves three steps:

a) Specification of the application
This step is concerned with defining the general characteristics of the application, that is:

- the application name
- the date of creation
- the creator
- the version number
- the date of the last modification
- the directory in which the file containing the application specifications will be stored
- the application title.

The specification of these characteristics is made by filling in the fields of a form as in SQL*Forms. Some fields have default values like the date or the version number. Moving from one field to another is via the [Next Field] function key.

b) Specification of application users
This step allows the following definitions:

- the user class; each class is designated by a number
- the users who may use it
- which users belong to which class
- additional facilities that each user may enjoy, such as access to the BGM menu or activation of system commands from the menu.

c) Specification of the different menus
This step consists of defining individually each menu in the application. The specification of each menu is divided into three stages:

c1 – general menu specification, by providing:

- the menu name
- the top title
- the subtitle
- the bottom title, and
- a brief description of the role of the menu.

c2 – specification of menu options, for each option, give:

- the order number
- the class of user that may access it
- the associated text
- the associated command
- the type of the command.

c3 – specification of help messages. A help message may be defined for each option.

d) Saving the defined menus
This step consists of storing all the definitions in a file which is called a 'library'.

e) Menu generation
For the menus of an application to become executable, the file generated in the previous step d) has to be compiled. This step must also be carried out each time a modification is made to one of the menus.

13.2.5 Generating documentation for an application

SQL*Menu can provide detailed documentation in summary form for all the existing applications.

This documentation contains:
• a list of all the menus
• a list of all the options
• a list of the user classes
• lists of users
• help messages.

The documentation is generated first. It can then be displayed on the screen or printed out.

13.2.6 Administration of SQL*Menu

The administration of SQL*Menu can be undertaken by anyone who has the DBA privilege. It consists of:

• creating users, assigning them to a class and attributing their privileges
• using the utility for translating menus
• defining the characteristics of terminals and in particular the function keys
• controlling the 'library' files.

The administrator can also carry out operations on the generated applications, such as renaming the whole application, renaming menus, deleting applications or deleting menus.

14 Data Administration

14.1 Introduction

Data administration consists of defining the database and ensuring that it is properly used. Just as a database may be seen as existing on three levels (external, design and internal), so the administration is also carried out on three levels. At the design level, the role of the administrator is to define (or at least participate in the definition) of the conceptual schema of the database. He therefore designs the schemas of the different tables and the rules to be applied to these tables. At the external level, he decides who may access what, and how. He therefore controls the users and their access to the data. Finally, at the internal level, the role of the database administrator is to match the conceptual schema with the facilities of the DBMS so as to extract the optimum return in terms of performance, integrity and security.

Generally speaking, the database administrator has a dual role – organisational and technical. The organisational role concerns the definition of the conceptual schema of the database and the sharing of this data by the users. The technical role consists of implementing this schema and sharing the data using the technical facilities of the DBMS. The two roles may be carried out by one or more individuals.

In Oracle, any person who has the DBA privilege is considered to be a database administrator. When the system is installed, two users are automatically considered to be database administrators: SYS and SYSTEM. Only these two users may create other users and assign to them the DBA privilege. The passwords assigned during the installation to the SYS and SYSTEM users are respectively CHANGE_ON_INSTALL and MANAGER. For obvious security reasons, these passwords must be changed immediately after installation. The main difference between the SYS user and the SYSTEM user is that the first has access to the tables in the data dictionary, whereas the second only has access to the views of the dictionary. It is most advisable not to use the SYS account and especially not to alter its tables or add others to them.

In this chapter, we are interested purely in the technical aspects of administration. We will begin with a description of the internal structure of the database. We will then discuss the two means offered by Oracle for accelerating data access: indexes and clusters. We will then tackle the tools for guiding the system, such as start and stop, supervising the activities of users and the modification of terminal characteristics.

To restore the database to a coherent state after a failure, Oracle uses the journalisation technique. We will outline the principles of this technique before ending with some utilities employed by Oracle to save and restore a database or a part of that database and also be able to load a table from non-Oracle files.

An important part of the database administrator's role will not be discussed in this chapter: this is the creation of users and the control of their privileges. These were described in chapter 8.

14.2 Data storage

14.2.1 Structure of a database

A database is formed from one or more partitions. A partition is a logical unit that corresponds to one or more physical files.

The files and the partitions can be created and added to the database when the need for more space becomes apparent. On the other hand, they cannot be deleted. A partition called SYSTEM is automatically created for

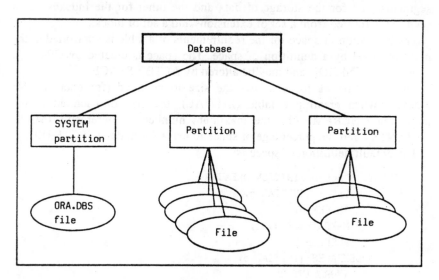

Figure 14.1 Structure of a single database

each database. It contains the tables of the data dictionary, the working tables and possibly the help tables. The file that corresponds to this partition is the one that is assigned to the DATABASE parameter in the INIT.ORA file.

A table can be physically held on several files belonging to the same partition. When an index is created for a table, it is stored in the partition of this table.

The following commands create files and partitions and add files to a partition.

- Creating a file

```
CCF file_name size
```

The size is expressed as a number of blocks.

- Creating a partition

```
CREATE PARTITION partition_name;
```

- Adding a file to a partition

```
ALTER PARTITION partition_name ADD FILE file_name;
```

The first command is an executable utility at the operating system level, whereas the last two are SQL*Plus commands.

14.2.2 *Table storage*

When a table is created, Oracle automatically reserves two spaces, called segments, one for the storage of data and the other for the indexes. Each segment is formed from a set of extensions and a set of blocks.

The allocation of space for the requirements of a table is controlled at the partition level by a definition of space. The space is created by CREATE SPACE DEFINITION and may be altered by ALTER SPACE.

The definition of space allows the size to be fixed (for data and for indexes) when creating a table (INITIAL), the size of each additional increment (INCREMENT), the maximum number of increments (MAX-EXTENTS), and the percentage of space to leave for updates (PCTFREE).

The default definition of space is:

```
CREATE SPACE DEFINITION DEFAULT
    DATAPAGES (INITIAL 5,
        INCREMENT 25,
        MAXEXTENTS 9999,
        PCTFREE 20)
    INDEXPAGES (INITIAL 5,
        INCREMENT 25,
        MAXEXTENTS 9999)
    PARTITION SYSTEM;
```

14.2.3 Block formats

The logical format of a block is shown in the following figure (describing non-cluster tables):

Date of last write	Type
Address of next block	
Address of preceding block	
Block heading	
Line number	Line length
id 1st column length	1st column
Data 1st column	
id 2nd column	Length 2nd column
Data 2nd column	
Ditto for other lines	
PCTFREE	
(unused space)	

The size of the Oracle block depends on the host size, generally it is 2048 or 4096 bytes. Oracle requires 76 bytes as overhead, leaving 1976 or 4020 for the data.

The operations that affect the distribution of space are insertion, updating and deletion.

In order to avoid overflow of a partition when carrying out a manipulation, the administrator must control memory occupation in the database. To do this, he can formulate the following two queries that provide information on:

- the number of empty adjacent blocks:

```
SELECT SPM$PID, SPM$ENDBLOCK - SPM$STARTBLOCK + 1
    FROM SYS.SPACEMAP;
```

The result appears as follows:

SPM$PID	SPM$ENDBLOCK-SPM$STARTBLOCK+1
1	2
1	30
1	40
1	0
1	69
1	100

This query gives for each partition identified by a number (1 denotes the SYSTEM partition), the number of empty blocks in each set of empty adjacent blocks. The sum of the values of the lines gives the total number of empty blocks in the database. To be able to create a table, there must be at least a set of adjacent blocks to contain the initial blocks of the table and extensions (see SPACE DEFINITION).

If the base is too fragmented, that is, if there are many empty blocks that are too dispersed, the database will have to be reorganised. This can be done by carrying out an import/export of the whole database, or selectively by copying and deleting tables.

- the average size of available space:

```
SELECT AVG(SPM$ENDBLOCK - SPM$STARTBLOCK + 1)"AVERAGE",
       MIN(SPM$ENDBLOCK - SPM$STARTBLOCK + 1)"MINIMUM",
       MAX(SPM$ENDBLOCK - SPM$STARTBLOCK + 1)"MAXIMUM",
       COUNT (*) "NB. EMPTY SPACES", SPM$PID "PARTITION"
FROM SYS.SPACEMAP
GROUPBY SPM$PID;
```

The result is of the form:

AVERAGE	MINIMUM	MAXIMUM	NB. EMPTY SPACES	PARTITION
41.8333333	2	100	6	1

The following are the results of exporting a user and then importing him.
  After export:

```
SELECT SPM$PID, SPM$ENDBLOCK - SPM$STARTBLOCK + 1 FROM
SYS.SPACEMAP;
```

SPM$PID	SPM$ENDBLOCK - SPM$STARTBLOCK + 1
1	2
1	110
1	69
1	70

14.2.4 Determining the number of data and index blocks

Determining the number of data blocks.
  The following are some recommendations for the use of space allocation:

- it is preferable to have a few large size extensions than to have many small size extensions
- the presence of columns having NULL values at the start that will subsequently take NOT NULL values requires a larger PCTFREE.

This results from the fact that NULL values occupy no physical space
- the creation of a table requires the availability of initial space in the form of adjacent blocks.

Estimating the initial size may take account of the following elements:

- number of lines in a table
- average length of variable length data
- the percentage of NULL data in each column
- total number of alterations, especially those that increase the size of lines.

The formula that gives the number of blocks is:

```
B = R/RB
B : number of logical blocks required for the table
R : number of lines in the table
RB = integer part of (1-F) * (S-H) / BR
BR = average number of bytes per line
   = SUMi (1-Ni) * (Ci+K+I) + L + Q
Ci : average length of each column
Ni : fraction of the ith column with the value NULL
F : PCTFREE
```

The value I, K, L, S and H are system specific and depend on the version of Oracle. They designate:

```
K : indicator for column length
I : column id
L : line length
Q : sequence number in the line
S : logical size of Oracle block
H : header per block.
```

14.3 Accelerators

The Oracle system contains two means whereby the user may improve access speed to the database. These are indexes and clusters.

14.3.1 Indexes

Indexes, similar to those normally found at the end of manuals, assist the user in localising information more rapidly. They are physically independent of data, and may also be deleted and recreated at any time.

The owner of a table, or anyone who has the INDEX privilege to this table, may create an index. It will be used when accessing data independently of the user who created it.

The following command creates an index:

```
CREATE [UNIQUE] INDEX index_name
    ON table_name (column_name [ASC | DESC],...)
    [COMPRESS | NOCOMPRESS]
    [SYSSORT | NOSYSSORT]
    [ROWS = n]
    [PCTFREE = {20 | n}];
```

SYSSORT|NOSYSSORT : only SYSSORT, the sort algorithm adopted by Oracle, may be used. The default is to use SYSSORT.

ROWS : not used.

PCTFREE = n : the rate of filling of the leaves of the B+tree when indexes were created. A value of between 10 and 15 per cent is reasonable.

COMPRESS/NOCOMPRESS : the index data is to be compressed or not.

The UNIQUE option ensures the uniqueness of lines. Two lines may not have the same value for the column(s) used by the index. This is the method often used to implement the concept of a key that does not exist explicitly in Oracle.

The CREATE INDEX command causes the indexed columns to be sorted, and the index blocks are organised into a B+tree. The organisation of the latter is done in such a way that each level of the tree contains an index for the next lower level. Thus the root block contains an index value and the addresses of the index blocks of the level below. Each leaf block in the tree contains the index value and its ROWID.

The main advantage of the B+tree organisation is that it takes perceptibly the same time to access any element in it (balanced tree).

A table may have several indexes at once. A balance has to be found between the number of indexes and the overhead penalty caused by updating them.

An index may relate to several columns, in which it still preserves the uniqueness across the columns used. It also helps to bring improved performance to queries that involve selection from several columns.

A query with several predicates can use multiple indexes if:

- the indexes do not have the UNIQUE designation
- the predicates are equalities
- and the predicates are defined on the same table.

In this case, the partial results that come from each index are merged to determine the definitive result. Oracle can use the properties of indexes (compress/noncompress, unique/non-unique) and the characteristics of columns to decide which index to take and so avoid the merging operation.

Whether or not to use an index is decided by the Oracle optimiser. This is based on the following choices:

The index is not used if:

- there is no WHERE clause in the query
- the predicate alters the value of the indexed column with a function or with an arithmetic operation
- the search includes a NULL value comparison condition on the indexed column.

The index is used if:

- the index column is found in the WHERE clause
- and the indexed column has not been changed.

14.3.2 Clusters

Clustering has the aim of physically bringing together data that is often logically accessed together. This has the following advantages:

- it reduces the access time because the data is physically close
- storage space is reduced because data common to several tables is stored once only.

It should be noted that the existence and use of clusters are transparent to the user.

- Creation

```
CREATE CLUSTER cluster_name
    (column_name type [NOT NULL[,...)
    [SIZE n]
    [SPACE space_name]
    [COMPRESS|NOCOMPRESS];
```

SIZE : the size in bytes of a logical block, its value must be a divisor of the size of a physical block.

Determining the size of the logical block depends on the number of lines to be grouped by value of the key and the average length of these lines.

A cluster may contain two or more tables. The tables are placed in the cluster by the CREATE TABLE command.

A cluster is formed from a name and a list of columns. One or more of these columns must be in the tables that will be placed in the cluster. They must therefore have the same data type and the same length.

For all the tables in the cluster, the lines having the same value in the cluster column are grouped together in the same logical block.

14.4 Tools for operating the system

In this section we will describe the database administrator's tasks for operating the system. They concern:

- starting and stopping the system : IOR utility
- controlling the size of the SGA zone : SGI utlility
- controlling the system activity : ODS
- altering the characteristics of a terminal : CRT.

14.4.1 Starting and stopping the system (IOR)

The IOR command starts up and closes down the system. The option used with this command determines which of these operations occurs. There are two possible types of start : warm start and cold start. Stop may also be carried out in two ways: sudden stop without warning users and progressively by waiting for all users to disconnect. Every activation of the IOR command causes the INIT.ORA file to be accessed; this contains the configuration parameters.

• *Starting Oracle*
The following command is used:

```
IOR start_mode [DBA][PFILE = parameters_file][SHARED][LIST]
```

The DBA option indicates that, for this session, only those users with the DBA privilege may connect. This is useful for carrying out administrative operations on the database, such as saving or restoring.

The PFILE argument fixes the file containing the start parameters. The INIT.ORA file is the default.

The option SHARED is usable with systems that allow partition sharing such as VMS. It may only be used with a warm start.

The option LIST causes the parameters of the parameter file to be displayed (INIT.ORA or the file specified in PFILE). This option may be used at both start up and close down. It can even be used by itself.

The start mode allows it to be stated whether it is a warm or a cold start. It may take one of the following parameters:

I[NIT] [NOCONFIRM] : This is the cold start. It initialises the database. Any uncommitted transactions of previous sessions are lost, and previous users are logged off. The NOCONFIRM option casuses the database to be initialised without asking for confirmation.

W[ARM] : This is the Oracle warm start. It opens the different files of the database, activates the different processes, cancels incomplete transactions from the previous session and deletes any temporary tables. With this start, information about the SGA is displayed, such as:

- size in bytes of the fixed data
- size in bytes of the variable data
- database buffers.

• *Stopping Oracle*
The following command is used:
IOR stop_mode [LIST]
   The LIST option has the same meaning as during the start.
   The stop mode allows specification of an immediate stop or a progressive stop. It may take one of the following parameters:

C[LEAR] : This option causes the immediate halt of Oracle. All processes are stopped without warning the users. Any transactions in operation are interrupted and will be cancelled by the next warm start of Oracle.

S[HUT] : This initiates a progressive halt of the system. It refuses any new attempt to connect, but it allows existing users to terminate their sessions. Assigned transactions are committed. When all the users have disconnected and their transactions have been committed, the processes are halted and all the files are closed.

• *The parameter file (INIT.ORA)*
This file contains a set of parameters necessary for starting the system. The values assigned to these parameters can affect the system performance. The main parameters are:

– processes	maximum number of concurrent processes
– buffers	number of data buffers in main memory (50 by default)
– database	name of first file in the SYSTEM partition (ORACLE.DBS by default)
– before_image	name of before image file (ORACLE.BI by default)
– users	maximum number of users referenced by SQL commands.

Here is an example of the parameter values of the INIT.ORA file:

processes	30
buffers	50
database	oracle.dbs
before_image	oracle.bi
users	30.

   The complete list of parameters and their possible values is given in the Oracle manuals.

14.4.2 Controlling the size of the SGA (SGI)

The System Global Area (SGA) is a shared zone of the central or virtual memory allocated when the system starts up. It is the Oracle work zone. Its size is a function of the parameters in the INIT.ORA file or its equivalent.

The SGI utility is a tool that allows the size of the SGA to be measured from different parameter files. The syntax is:
SGI [PFILE = parameter_file] [LIST] [DETAIL]

As in the IOR command, the PFILE option indicates the parameter file. The default is the INIT.ORA file.

The inclusion of the LIST option causes the list of parameter values to be displayed. Both the default parameters and those defined in the parameter file are displayed.

The DETAIL option displays the total size in bytes used for some parameters. In its absence, the following information is displayed:

- size of fixed data
- size of variable data
- size of before_image buffers
- size of database buffers.

14.4.3 Oracle Display System (ODS)

The Oracle Display System utility ODS is a diagnostic tool for the system. At any time it will show:

- the processes (users) using Oracle
- the tools used by the different processes
- the tables used
- the state of the before_image file
- the input/output flow.

This information is displayed on the screen and may if required be stored in a file that we shall call a trace file. The facility is useful for evaluating the system and analysing its behaviour under varying conditions.

The ODS command activates this utility. It begins by displaying a first screen bearing the version number and inviting the selection of the information required. To obtain the list of available commands together with a short description of each, the user keys '?'. The list is:

Help (or ?)	displays all available commands
Bi	displays statistics on the before_image file
Close	closes the trace file

Cycle n	assigns n seconds to the display cycle
Exit	quits ODS
Io	displays the input/output flow
Locks (O)	displays the list of locks (O = all locks)
Open file	opens the trace file
Summary	displays a summary of Oracle activity
Table	displays the tables used by each user
User [idp1][idp2]	displays the activity of one, several or all the users identified by their process numbers.

The choice from among these commands is made by keying the appropriate name or just the uppercase letters as shown. Once the choice is made, the chosen screen is displayed. The Oracle manuals contain a detailed description of these screens.

14.4.4 Altering the characteristics of a terminal (CRT)

Some Oracle tools, such as SQL*Forms and SQL*Calc, use function keys and require certain display characteristics. The CRT utility alters the characteristics of a terminal (function keys and display mode). It also allows others to be created.

This utility uses tables called CRT tables that contain information specific to the terminal to generate files (with the CRT extension) that can be used by other programs. Each file constitutes a terminal definition.

Oracle contains a set of terminal definitions with one default, known as DEFAULT.CRT. The latter matches the most widespread types, such as IBM 3270 and VT100.

Altering or creating a terminal definition can be done in two ways:

- by executing the CRT form from SQL*Forms
- by directly altering the CRT tables using SQL*Plus.

14.5 Journalising

An essential requirement of any DBMS is the ability to recover after a breakdown. When a fault that damages the database occurs, it must be able to return to the most recent coherent state.

Oracle relies on the journalising mechanism to ensure that this feature is present by using a tool called AIJ (After Image Journalising). AIJ writes all the updates belonging to a transaction to a suite of files (journals) before making them effective in the database.

It should be noted that the journal may grow very rapidly given that AIJ writes the whole altered block even if the update only affected one byte.

Filling the journal files is carried out in a circular manner. When a file is full, it must be saved (manually or automatically by program), then it is refreshed in order to be reused.

To be able to apply journals, it is necessary to:

- save the database periodically when it is in a coherent state. Saving involves the database itself and the journal files
- ignore the journal files created before the save.

After a breakdown, AIJ will be used to apply the contents of the journals to the last save.

Journals are handled in two phases. The first eliminates transactions that have never been validated. In the second phase, the blocks that have not been eliminated by the first phase will be applied to the database.

14.6 Saving and restoring data

We will conclude this chapter on administration by describing the three utilities that are generally used by a database administrator, but may also be used by any other user.

These utilities allow one to:

- save objects controlled by Oracle so that they may later be recovered in the same database or in other Oracle databases
- load into a database objects that come from a previous save of the same database or of other Oracle databases
- load tables from files that contain data from other applications.

The first operation is called export and the utility is called EXPORT. The second operation is called import and uses the IMPORT utility. The third is carried out by the Oracle utility ODL (Oracle Data Loader).

Figure 14.2 illustrates how these utilities are used.

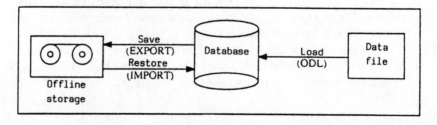

Figure 14.2 Import, export and loading of data

14.6.1 Saving data (EXPORT)

The EXPORT utility makes copies of the following objects in a database:

- table definitions
- table data
- privileges assigned to users
- definitions of views, synonyms and spaces
- indexes
- clusters.

These objects are stored in a system file that can later be recovered to reload the same database or other databases. As we have seen in section 14.2, saving and then restoring a database frees memory space.

The EXPORT utility can be used in three modes:

• *User mode*
This mode allows the saving of table and data definitions, clusters, index privileges and space definitions of a given user. If this mode is activated by a user, only the objects that belong to him are saved. If activated by a database administrator, the save can apply to several users.

• *Table mode*
This mode only allows the saving of table definitions and data and space definitions. For the user without the DBA privilege, only the tables that he owns may be saved. A database administrator can save any user's tables.

• *Database mode*
This mode allows the saving of the following objects: table definitions and data, index, clusters, privileges, views, synonyms and space definitions. Only the database administrator may use this mode.

To run the save, the command is:
EXP [user/pass_word]

Oracle then asks a series of questions that the user must answer. A default reply is given for each question. If the user simply responds with carriage returns, the default answer is accepted.

The EXPORT utility may only be activated by users who have the RESOURCE privilege or DBA.

14.6.2 Restoring data (IMPORT)

The IMPORT utility allows the loading into a database of the whole or a part of a back up file. Objects copied during the save operation are restored into the database.

The IMPORT command activates the utility:

```
IMP [user/pass_word]
```

As for the EXPORT utility, the system asks questions for which there are default responses. The questions are:

- name of saved file
- size of buffer
- if you wish to have a list of the contents of the saved file
- if an error on creating an object prevents the loading of lines from a table or not
- if you wish to import privileges
- if you wish to import table lines
- if you wish to import the complete security file.

To be able to execute the IMPORT utility, the user must have the RESOURCE and CONNECT privilege. He must also be able to access the security files.

14.6.3 Loading tables from non-Oracle files

The ODL (Oracle Data Loader) utility copies into an existing table data taken from non-Oracle files. The operations that are possible are:

- loading all the data in the file
- loading some of the data in the file
- loading only into certain columns in a table
- automatic generation of numeric keys.

The ODL utility uses two types of file as input: a control file and one or more data files. As output, it produces a log file of the loaded records and perhaps a file of unloadable data records. Figure 14.3 shows the interaction between ODL and the different files.

We will now examine the role and format of each of these files.

a) The control file

This file describes the format of records of the data file(s), the table to be loaded, as well as its columns and the match between the record fields and the columns. Three commands make up this file:

```
- DEFINE RECORD
```

defines the format of records in the data file. Its syntax is:

```
DEFINE RECORD record_name AS
    field_name (type [LOC (position)])...;
```

The LOC clause defines the position of a field in the record. The first

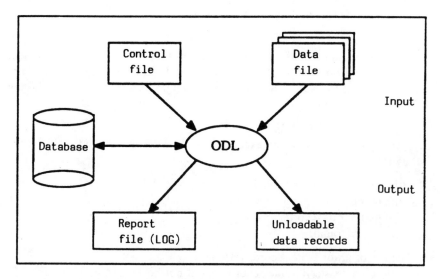

Figure 14.3 Process of loading a table

character corresponds to position O. The position may be absolute (unsigned number) or relative to the preceding field (signed number).

The possible types are: FLOAT, INTEGER and CHAR.

- DEFINE SOURCE

defines the data file(s). It takes the following form:

```
DEFINE SOURCE source_name
       FROM file1 [files2...]
       LENGTH length
       CONTAINING record_name;
```

The source name is any symbolic name. The FROM clause indicates the data file(s), the LENGTH clause gives the length of the record. Finally, the CONTAINING clause indicates the name of the record assigned to the file. It is the same name used in the DEFINE RECORD command.

- FOR EACH

describes the operation of inserting the data into the table. Its form is:

```
FOR EACH RECORD
    INSERT INTO table_name (column,...)
    VALUES (field,...)
NEXT RECORD;
```

The table_name is the name of the table into which the data is to be inserted. The fields in the VALUES clause are either constants or fields defined in the DEFINE RECORD command.

b) The data file
This file corresponds to the whole or a part of the source data. Its form must be identical with that described in the DEFINE RECORD command of the control file. All the fields must be of fixed length except the last which may have a variable length.

c) The summary file (LOC)
It contains a summary of the execution of the ODL utility and includes the following:

- the number of records read
- the number of records rejected
- the number of records loaded
- the errors found.

d) The file of unloadable records (BAD)
This file only exists if some records could not be loaded into the table. In this case, it contains all the unloadable records. These records can be corrected and the file will then be used as a data file.

Execution of the ODL utility is carried out with the following command:

```
ODL control_file summary_file
    [user/pass_word] [-options]
```

The options used are:

Sn : ignore the n first records
Ln : load n records
Cn : validate the insertion for every n records, default n = 100
En : only stop the process after finding n errors, default n = 50
Bn : size of buffer used.

15 Version 6 of Oracle

15.1 Introduction

Version 6 of Oracle represents an important stage in the evolution of this product. Although it is functionally very similar to the previous version, version 6 may be considered to be a new product to the extent that more than 75 per cent of the kernel has been rewritten to take into account the constraints imposed by the evolution of the market. Relational systems have in fact acquired a technical maturity that now enables one to envisage their being used for 'heavy' applications such as transaction processing. This nonetheless requires some adaptation to obtain the level of performance and security that such applications demand.

Version 6 of Oracle is designed to provide an efficient solution to these constraints by offering:

- a high transaction rate
- improved response times
- a better tolerance of 'crashes'
- the possibility of controlling large databases, etc.

These improvements have been obtained by a complete recasting of the product. The global architecture has been rethought in order to optimise use of both the CPU and I/O operations. Transaction management has been reviewed and concurrent access to data is now controlled by a locking mechanism whose granule is now the line and no longer the whole table.

The physical structure of the database has been redefined and new tools are available to the database administrator.

All of these modifications now combine to make Oracle version 6 a high performance system suited to the new constraints that it must deal with.

15.2 General architecture

The general architecture of Oracle version 6 differs from that of version 5 through the addition of a new layer: the PL/SQL layer. This extends the SQL layer by offering the possibility of combining procedural constructs with SQL commands. It allows variables to be declared and assigned, cursors to be used, and control structures like conditions, loops, etc to be built.

15.3 Internal architecture

Figure 15.1 shows the internal architecture of Oracle version 6. It is arranged on three levels:

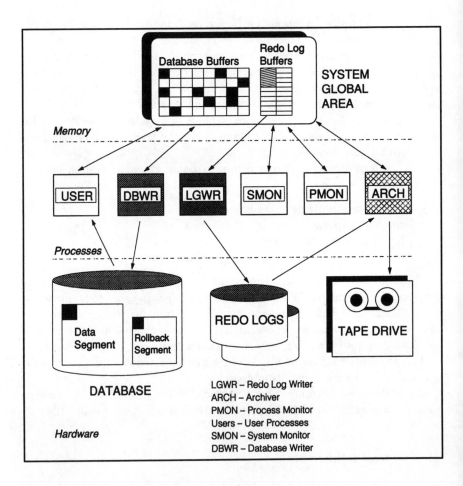

Figure 15.1 Internal architecture of Oracle version 6

- file level
- process level
- memory level.

The first level corresponds to the structure of the database and the way in which the data is stored. It comprises the database, one or more pilot or control files, journalising files and archive support. The process level corresponds to the different Oracle processes that ensure the management of data. It includes a number of server and user processes. Finally, the memory level corresponds to the organisation of data so far as the central memory is concerned. It consists of a memory area called SGA (System Global Area) containing buffers assigned to the server processes and cursors assigned to the user processes.

15.3.1 File level

An Oracle database is arranged in different logical and physical levels. Figure 15.2 shows this arrangement.

Database	<db_name>						
TABLESPACES	<SYSTEM>				<TS1>		
Files	<Oracle1.dbs>		<Oracle2.dbs>		<Oracle3.dbs>		
Segments	Data	Index	Rollback	Data	Temporary	Index	Data
Extensions	1	1	1 ¦ 2	1 ¦ 2 ¦ 3	1 ¦ 2	1	1

Figure 15.2 Logical and physical arrangement of a database

On the first level we find the database. This consists of a number of logical units called TABLESPACEs. Each TABLESPACE is physically formed from system files in which are stored data (temporary and permanent), indexes and information concerning possible ROLLBACKs. These files are divided into segments, each of which is a sequence of extensions (EXTENT).

Concept of a database

In the preceding versions of Oracle, the concept of the database was implicit. All the data handled by Oracle made up a database. This database was not named and there was no command to manipulate databases. One of the new features of version 6 is the possibility of creating and manipulating a database. A database is identified by a name and it is logically made up of one or more TABLESPACEs. Section 15.4.1 below contains the commands for manipulating databases.

Concept of TABLESPACE

The concept of TABLESPACE constitutes the logical support for the storage of different objects in the database (tables, index, clusters, etc). It is the equivalent of the concept of partition in version 5. Each TABLESPACE is identified by a name. A database must have at least one TABLESPACE called SYSTEM. A TABLESPACE is made up logically from one or more segments and physically from one or more files. Each object in the database (table, index, cluster, etc) must always appear in a single TABLESPACE.

The TABLESPACE constitutes the most detailed administration level of a database. It is thus possible to activate or deactivate a TABLESPACE without halting Oracle (to save or restore an individual TABLESPACE). A TABLESPACE can also be deleted even if it contains data. Section 15.4.2 contains the commands for controlling TABLESPACEs.

Concept of a file

A file constitutes the physical support for storing data. There are three types of file: database files, recovery files and control files.

Database files contain database data, the dictionary, indexes, etc.

Recovery files (REDO LOG) number at least two. They provide protection for the database in the event of a hardware or software crash by recording all modifications made to the database and applying them subsequently. The REDO LOG files are used in circular fashion. Each file contains the following information:

- identification of the transaction
- block number
- line number
- column number
- new value.

Pilot or control file(s) (CONTROL FILE). There must be at least one control file in order to be able to start the database; however, it is advisable to have several copies on different supports for security. Each file contains the necessary information to run the system (database name, date and time that the files were created, etc).

Concept of segment
A segment is the logical location that corresponds to an object. It is entirely contained in the same TABLESPACE. When a segment is deleted, the freed space is returned to the database. Each segment has a name and segment type. There are four types of segment:

- Data segments. They store data:
  - user tables
  - system tables (data dictionary)
  - tables grouped as clusters.
- Index segments. They store index data separately from data segments. Each index is contained in a distinct segment.
- Temporary segments. These segments are created temporarily by Oracle to carry out explicit sorts (ORDER BY in a query) or implicit sorts (creating an index, GROUP BY, etc). They are deleted at the end of the transaction that created them.
- Rollback segments. They contain before images to enable transactions to be cancelled and allow return to a previous state. It is the equivalent to the before_image files of version 5. They contain the following information:
  - transaction identifier
  - block number
  - line number
  - column number
  - old value.

Concept of EXTENT
An extension is a contiguous allocation of space in a segment. It must be entirely contained within the same file. The initial size and the amount of increment are determined by the INITIAL and PCTINCREASE parameter of the STORAGE clause (see section 15.4.3). This size may not be less than 4096 bytes nor greater than 4095 megabytes.

15.3.2 *Memory level*

The memory is made up of areas called System Global Area (SGA) and Process Global Area (PGA).

The SGA is an area of memory common to all Oracle processes. It is created during start-up of the database. It consists of:

- dictionary cache containing frequently used data
- integrity mechanisms (locks, latches)
- information about processes
- database buffers:
  - data blocks
  - index blocks
  - ROLLBACK segment blocks
  - temporary segment blocks
- REDO LOG buffers that contain the following information:
  - transaction identifier
  - record containing what has changed in a line
  - records containing terminated transactions.

The PGA is formed from cursors. It contains:

- the SQL query
- the compiled query (in the form of routine calls)
- a record of the result.

15.3.3 Process level

The architecture of Oracle version 6 is made up of the following processes:
REDO LOG WRITER (LGWR)
This process writes the contents of the REDO LOG buffers of the SGA area
into the REDO LOG files when

- a commit is made
- there is no longer room in SGA for the REDO LOG buffers
- the DBWR requests it.

DATABASE WRITER (DBWR)

This process carries out the deferred writing of the blocks modified in the
database. This writing is carried out when:

- the SGA buffers are full
- control points (CHECKPOINT) are carried out.

This process is initiated every three seconds to rewrite the least frequently
used buffers.
The operation of DBWR can be controlled by certain parameters of
INIT.ORA.

PROCESS MONITOR (PMON)

This frees those resources (SGA, locks) monopolised by a user process that
terminated badly and cancels invalid transactions.

SYSTEM MONITOR (SMON)
When the database is retrieved, it clears any incomplete transactions. It also clears any unused temporary segments.

ARCHIVER (ARCH)
This copies the inactive REDO LOG files to disk or to tape (usable if there is a crash). This process is optional and it works asynchronously compared with other processes.

15.4 Data definition

The main new features of Oracle version 6 so far as SQL is concerned relate to the definition of data. Some commands are new compared with version 5, while others have undergone some changes. The new commands concern the control of the database, TABLESPACEs and SEQUENCEs. The introduction of these new concepts has an effect on the old commands for defining data controlling tables, clusters and indexes.

15.4.1 Database control

The concept of the database is one of the chief novelties of version 6. In previous versions, all the tables controlled by Oracle made up an implicit database. There were therefore no commands concerned with defining databases. In version 6 it is possible to create and modify a database. There is no command to delete a database.

The command to create a database consists of assigning a name to the new database and defining its characteristics.

```
CREATE DATABASE database_name
    [CONTROLFILE [REUSE]]
    [LOGFILE file_specification [,file_specification]...]
    [MAXLOGFILES n]
    [DATAFILE file_specification [,file_specification]...]
    [MAXDATAFILES n]
    [MAXINSTANCES n]
    [ARCHIVELOG|NOARCHIVELOG]
    [SHARED|EXCLUSIVE];
```

Where 'file_specification' = 'file_name' [SIZE n [K|M]][REUSE]
K and M signify that the size is expressed in kilobytes or megabytes. The underlined options are the defaults if no specification is made.

The LOGFILE clause specifies the list of REDO LOG files.

The DATAFILE clause contains the list of data files.

Clauses MAXLOGFILES and MAXDATAFILES specify respectively the maximum number of REDO LOG and data files.

When the ARCHIVELOG option is present the archive mode is automatically triggered as soon as the database is opened up.

When the EXCLUSIVE option is specified the database cannot be shared by several users.

The command for modifying a database allows some of its characteristics to be altered. It allows REDO LOG files to be added, deleted or renamed, the ARCHIVELOG mode to be activated or deactivated, and the database to be mounted, dismounted, opened or closed.

The syntax of this command is:

```
ALTER DATABASE database_name
    [ADD LOGFILE file_specification [,file_specification]...]
    [DROP LOGFILE 'file_name' [,'file_name']...]
    [RENAME LOGFILE 'file_name' [,'file_name']
      TO 'file_name' [,'file_name']...]
    [ARCHIVELOG|NOARCHIVELOG]
    [MOUNT [SHARED|EXCLUSIVE]|DISMOUNT]
    [OPEN|CLOSE [NORMAL|IMMEDIATE]];
```

15.4.2 Control of TABLESPACEs

The concept of a TABLESPACE was introduced in section 15.3.1. Here we are concerned with the commands for creating, modifying and deleting TABLESPACEs.

The command to create a TABLESPACE consists of assigning it a name and defining its characteristics.

```
CREATE TABLESPACE ts_name
    DATAFILE file_specification [,file_specification]...
    [DEFAULT STORAGE storage_clause]
    [ONLINE|OFFLINE];
```

The file_specification has the same meaning and syntax as in the command for creating a database. The DATAFILE clause gives the list of data files contained in the TABLESPACE. The OFFLINE option makes the TABLESPACE inaccessible (until modified by ALTER TABLESPACE). ONLINE is the default.

storage_clause defines the memory space parameters for the TABLESPACE. Its syntax is:

```
storage_clause = [INITIAL n]
                 [NEXT n]
                 [MINEXTENTS n]
                 [MAXEXTENTS n]
                 [PCTINCREASE n]
```

where

```
INITIAL     : size in bytes of the first extension
NEXT        : size in bytes of an increment
MINEXTENTS  : minimum number of extensions (on creation)
MAXEXTENTS  : maximum number of extensions
PCTINCREASE : percentage increase of NEXT compared with the
previous allocation.
```

The following command deletes the TABLESPACE:

```
DROP TABLESPACE ts_name
   [INCLUDING CONTENTS];
```

When the INCLUDING CONTENTS option is included the TABLESPACE is deleted even if it contains data.

The command for modifying TABLESPACE allows new data files to be added (DATAFILE), existing ones to be renamed, memory space parameters to be altered and the option ONLINE/OFFLINE to be switched.

The syntax is:

```
ALTER TABLESPACE ts_name
[ADD DATAFILE file_specification [,file_specification]..]
[RENAME DATAFILE 'file_name' [,'file_name']...]
   TO 'file_name' [,'file_name']...]
[DEFAULT STORAGE storage_clause]
[ONLINE|OFFLINE [NORMAL|IMMEDIATE]]
[BEGIN BACKUP|END BACKUP];
```

The BEGIN BACKUP and END BACKUP options trigger and stop the save mechanism (see 15.7.2).

15.4.3 Control of SEQUENCEs

One of the limitations of the Oracle system in its previous versions was the absence of an automatic sequence generator. This concept is often necessary for the control of certain data. Software developers had to see to it themselves when they found the need for it.

Version 6 takes care of this control. It allows an arithmetic sequence of numbers to be generated. The user defines the characteristics of the sequence that is to be stored in the data dictionary like any other object in the database. This sequence can then be used concurrently by different users.

The command for creating a sequence consists of giving it characteristics. It has the following syntax:

```
CREATE SEQUENCE sequence_name
    [INCREMENTED BY incr_val]
    [START WITH init_val]
    [MINVALUE min_val |NOMINVALUE]
    [MAXVALUE max_val |NOMAXVALUE]
    [CYCLE|NOCYCLE]
    [ORDER|NOORDER]
    [CACHE cach_val |NOCACH];
```

sequence_name is the name that identifies the sequence
init_val is the initial value assigned to the sequence (default 1)
incr_val is the increment value between two successive elements in the sequence (default 1)
min_val and max_val are respectively the minimum and maximum values that the sequence may take (default 1 and 10e27).

When the CYCLE option is specified, the sequence returns to the initial value as soon as the maximum value is reached.

This command may only be executed by a user who has the RESOURCE privilege.

Like other objects in the database, a sequence may only be used by users who have obtained a GRANT SELECT on this sequence.

A sequence definition may be modified with the command ALTER SEQUENCE. All the parameters (or options) can be altered except the initial value (START WITH).

A sequence definition can also be deleted with the DROP SEQUENCE command.

The sequence definitions are stored in the following dictionary views:

```
USER_SEQUENCES for user sequences
ALL_SEQUENCES for public sequences.
```

Using sequences

A value of a sequnce is a numerical value that may be assigned to a numerical field. It is chiefly used in the UPDATE (SET clause) and INSERT (VALUES clause) commands.

Each sequence has two pseudo-columns assigned to it:

```
CURVAL  : current value of the sequence
NEXTVAL : next value of the sequence
```

NEXTVAL is used when it is required to increment the sequence and use the new value, whereas CURVAL is used to refer to the current value of the sequence.

These pseudo-columns must be prefixed with the sequence name (seq_name CURVAL or seq_name NEXTVAL). When the sequence has been created by another user, the sequence name must be prefixed with the user's name (user.seq_name CURVAL).

15.4.4 Control of tables

For the control of tables, only the commands for creating and modifying the structure of tables have changed in comparison with version 5. The delete command (DROP TABLE) remains unchanged.

```
CREATE TABLE table_name
    (column_specification [,column_specification]...)
    [PCTUSED n] [PCTFRE n]
    [TABLESPACE ts_name]
    [INITRANS n] [MAXTRANS n]
    [STORAGE storage_clause]
    [CLUSTER cluster_name (column_name [,column_name]...)]
    [AS SELECT query];
```

The specification of columns and the clauses PCTUSED, PCTFREE, CLUSTER and AS SELECT have the meaning as those of version 5.

The TABLESPACE clause allows specification of the TABLESPACE in which the table will be created. The default is TABLESPACE SYSTEM.

The INITRANS clause determines the minimum number of concurrent transactions on a block (default 1, minimum 1, maximum 255).

The MAXTRANS clause determines the maximum number of concurrent transactions on a block (default 255, minimum 1, maximum 255).

The STORAGE clause has the same syntax as that described in 15.4.2.

The command for modifying the table structure (ALTER TABLE) allows the modifiable space parameters to be changed, except for TABLESPACE, INITIAL and MINEXTENTS. As in version 5, it also allows columns to be added or the size of existing columns to be increased.

15.4.5 Control CLUSTERs

As with the control of tables, only the command for creating and modifying clusters has changed in comparison with version 5. The difference lies in the use of TABLESPACEs and in the number of concurrent transactions per block.

The new syntax of the cluster creation command is:

```
CREATE CLUSTER cluster_name
    (column_name type [,column_name type]...)
    [PCTUSED n][PCTFREE n}
    [INITRANS n][MAXTRANS n]
    [TABLESPACE ts_name]
    [STORAGE storage_clause]
    [SIZE n];
```

The options and clauses have the same meaning as the command CREATE TABLE.

As with the modification of table structure, the command ALTER CLUSTER allows all the modifiable parameters to be changed, except for TABLESPACE, INITIAL and MINEXTENTS.

15.4.6 Control of indexes

The new syntax of the index creation command is:

```
CREATE [UNIQUE] INDEX index_name ON
    table_name (column_name [ASC|DESC][,column_name]...)
    CLUSTER cluster_name
    [PCTFREE n]
    [TABLESPACE ts_name]
    [STORAGE storage_clause]
    [NOSORT];
```

15.5 PL/SQL

PL/SQL is a procedural extension of the SQL language. Although often claimed as a strong point, the non-procedural character of the SQL language restricts the possibilities for formulating complex queries. For example, it is not possible to repeat a query or execute a query if a particular condition is satisfied.

With PL/SQL it is possible to program by combining SQL commands with PL/SQL commands. It is thus possible to:

- chain/concatenate queries and possibly exchange data
- use control structures similar to those of conventional programming languages (loops, conditions, etc)
- use typed variables
- use cursors.

A PL/SQL processing unit is called a block and has the following structure:

```
DECLARE
     Declaration of variables and cursors

BEGIN
     SQL and PL/SQL commands

EXCEPTION
     Error handling

END
```

The syntax for declaring variables is:
variable_name data_type;

The data type is any data type known to Oracle.

Declaration of cursors is done in the same way as for application programs (see PRO*C).

So far as the commands that follow the keyword BEGIN are concerned, they can be:

- SQL commands: SELECT, INSERT, UPDATE, DELETE, COMMIT, ROLLBACK, etc
- cursor manipulation commands: OPEN, FETCH and CLOSE
- PL/SQL commands: LOOP...EXIT WHEN...END LOOP.

The last part of a PL/SQL block is reserved for error handling. It allows provision to be made for action in the case of an error. The form of error handling commands is as follows:
WHEN error_condition SQL command;

A special error condition (OTHERS) allows provision to be made for handling all unspecified kinds of error.

15.6 Control of transactions and concurrent accesses

The new features of version 6, so far as transactions and concurrent accesses are concerned, involve the concept of a sub-transaction and some new types of locking.

15.6.1 Transactions and sub-transactions

We recall that a transaction is a logical processing unit which must be executed in its totality or not at all. There is no command to mark the start of a transaction. This start is implicitly the start of an Oracle session (connecting with the database) or the end of another transaction. As for the end of a transaction, it may cause either the verification of the operations carried out or their cancellation. Verification is made after:

- a COMMIT command
- a command to define data
- the normal end of a program with disconnection from Oracle.

A transaction is cancelled after:

- a ROLLBACK command
- an abnormal output/exit
- a normal end of a program without disconnection from Oracle
- a crash (disc, CPU, etc).

The concept of a sub-transaction, which did not exist in previous versions, allows processing units to be divided up more finely. A transaction may thus be divided into sub-transactions. So, in the event of an error (or any other event), it is possible to cancel just one part of the transaction.

The commands for controlling sub-transactions are:

```
SAVEPOINT sp_name
ROLLBACK TO sp_name
```

The first marks the start of a sub-transaction and the second cancels the sub-transaction sp_name.

Example

```
(connection)        -> start transaction 1
update ...
insert ...
SAVEPOINT sp        -> start sub-transaction
update ...
ROLLBACK TO sp      -> end sub-transaction (cancel update)
.
.
.
commit              -> end transaction 1 (verify)
                       start transaction 2
select ...
delete
.
.
(Exit)              -> end transaction 2 (verify)
```

This concept of a sub-transaction is especially useful in application programs that use subprograms (procedures, functions).

15.6.2 Concurrent accesses

To guarantee a pseudo-parallel execution of transactions, it is necessary for there to be fine control of concurrent accesses. In this way several transactions can be executed simultaneously to achieve a high level of performance. However, it is important to ensure that the pseudo-parallel execution of transactions gives the same result as a sequential execution. To achieve this, Oracle momentarily locks the data used by a transaction until the end of the update. Any other transactions requesting this data are made to wait. An important parameter that affects performance is that of the minimum volume of locked data, called a data granule.

Data can be locked explicitly by using the LOCK command, or it is locked implicitly. Implicit locking depends on two parameters of the INIT.ORA file. These are:

```
ROW-LOCKING = ALWAYS : Version 6 default
            = INTENT : Version 5 behaviour

SERIALISABLE = FALSE : default mode
             = TRUE : ANSI mode
```

The explicit lock command has the following syntax:

```
LOCK TABLE table_name IN lock_mode MODE [NOWAIT]
```

lock_mode can be one of the following:

```
EXCLUSIVE (X) : exclusive locking at table level
SHARE (S) : on data reading, the data is not updated
ROW SHARE (RS)/SHARE UPDATE : exclusive locking of lines for
                                  update
SHARE ROW EXCLUSIVE (SRX) : exclusive locking or update at
                                  table level
ROW EXCLUSIVE (RX) : exclusive locking or update at line
                         level.
```

There is a new command that allows a consistent read at the transaction level. This is the command

```
SET TRANSACTION READ ONLY
```

This order is the first in the transaction. The transaction may only have SELECT queries.

15.7 SQL*DBA administration utility

15.7.1 *Introduction*

All the data administration operations have been grouped within the
SQL*DBA utility. It includes the utilities IOR, ODS, CCF and AIJ of
version 5. It is also possible to activate SQL*Plus and PL/SQL commands,
with a few exceptions (edit, data formatting, DESCRIBE and COPY).

The following are the main SQL*DBA commands:

```
CONNECT :       connects to a database
DISCONNECT :    disconnects from a database
HOST :          executes an operating system level command, then
                returns to SQL*DBA
MONITOR :       supervises the evolution of the database in real
                time (process, users, locks, tables, statistics,
                etc)
ARCHIVELOG :    starts or stops the archive
RECOVER :       restores TABLESPACE or the whole database (cold
                start)
SHOW :          displays some information (process, user, etc)
STARTUP :       starts an already created database (mounting of the
                database, creation of the SGA, opening the database
                and control files)
SHUTDOWN :      closes and dismounts a database. This command may be
                executed with different options:
   NORMAL :     waits for all users to disconnect; no further
                connections are permitted. It is the equivalent of
                IOR SHUTDOWN of version 5.
   IMMEDIATE:   terminates those operations that are running and
                does not wait for all users to disconnect.
   ABORT :      stops all operations that are running. It is the
                equivalent of IOR CLEAR of version 5.
```

15.7.2 *Mechanisms for saving and restoring data*

There are two mechanisms for saving and restoring data. One is said to be
logical and the other physical. Logical saving and restoring are carried out
by means of the data import/export utility examined in chapter 14. We
recall that this operation may be carried out at different levels of granularity:
table, user or database. In the following we will concentrate on the physical
mechanism for saving and restoring.

The different types of save are:
– saving a closed or open database
– saving TABLESPACEs
– saving control files.

a) Saving a closed table
This is done on a previously closed table (SHUTDOWN NORMAL). Then, a save of the database, recovery and control files is made. After this save, the database can be reopened.

b) Saving an open database
It is possible to save a database when it is open and being manipulated by other users. This operation is more complicated than the previous one and requires certain precautions. It is carried out in the following stages:
– the ARCHIVELOG mode is activated with one of these two commands:

```
ARCHIVELOG START
```
or
```
ALTER DATABASE...ARCHIVELOG
```

– if the TABLESPACE containing the files is ONLINE, the following command is executed:

```
ALTER TABLESPACE ts_name
BEGIN BACKUP
```

This command is not necessary if the TABLESPACE is already OFFLINE
– the system command BACKUP is executed on the TABLESPACE files
– the end of the save is reported by means of the command:

```
ALTER TABLESPACE ts_name
END BACKUP
```

– the ARCHIVELOG mode is cancelled:

```
ALTER DATABASE db_name
NOARCHIVELOG
```

c) Saving a TABLESPACE
It is possible to save TABLESPACEs individually. This operation is done in the following stages:
– move to ARCHIVELOG mode
– execute the command

```
ALTER TABLESPACE ts_name
OFFLINE
```

– save the TABLESPACE
– execute the command

```
ALTER TABLESPACE ts_name
ONLINE
```

d) Saving the control file
It is advisable to save the CONTROL FILE systematically after every modification to the structure. This save is made using the command:

```
ALTER DATABASE BACKUP CONTROL FILE TO file_name
```

So far as restoration is concerned, the different types are:

– restoring a database
– restoring a TABLESPACE
– restoring the control file.

a) Restoring a database

This restore is only applicable to damaged database files. It goes through these stages:

– move to ARCHIVELOG mode
– mount the database in non-accessible mode:

```
STARTUP MOUNT db_name
```

– restore files with an operating system command
– execute the command:

```
RECOVER DATABASE
```

– open the database.

b) Restoring a TABLESPACE

Restoring a TABLESPACE (apart from SYSTEM) involves the following stages:

– move to ARCHIVELOG mode
– put TABLESPACE OFFLINE:

```
ALTER TABLESPACE ts_name OFFLINE
```

– restore all files of the TABLESPACE
– execute the command:

```
RECOVER TABLESPACE ts_name
```

– put TABLESPACE ONLINE:

```
ALTER TABLESPACE ts_name ONLINE
```

c) Restoring the control file

Restoring the control file is necessary when it is lost or invalidated. In this case, the procedure to be followed is:

– stop the database
– make the restore from a save of the control file or from another control file
– restart the database.

All these mechanisms for saving and restoring allow a cold start after crashes that have caused files to be lost.

A warm start can be achieved automatically with the STARTUP command after a sudden system stop that leaves the files intact.

Conclusion

In this book we have presented the Oracle database management system. The architecture of the system as well as the different functions have been described in order to facilitate their understanding and use.

We have tried to indicate the richness of the Oracle system tools which allow a wide variety of different types of application to be undertaken. This illustrates the advantage of relational systems for the improvement of productivity in the building of information systems.

In addition, Oracle have introduced a further software engineering tool to integrate with the CASE (Computer Aided Systems Engineering) technologies, and which constitutes a tool for building information systems.

Finally, with Oracle version 6 TPO (Transaction Processing Oriented), users now have a powerful tool for high volume transaction processing applications that extends further the range for this product.

Bibliography

Boyce, R.F. et al., 'Specifying queries as relational expressions: SQUARE', CACM, Vol. 18, 11, Nov. 1975, pp 621–628

Chamberlain, D.D. and Boyce, R.F., 'SEQUEL: A structured English query language', Proceedings of the ACM-CIGMOD Workshop on data description, access and control, 1974

Chamberlain, D.D. et al., 'SEQUEL2: A unified approach to data definition, manipulation and control', IBM Journal of Research and Development, Vol. 20, 6, 1976, pp 560–575

Codd, E.F., 'A relational model of data for large shared data banks', CACM, Vol. 13, 6, June 1970, pp 377–387

Date, C.S., *An introduction to database systems*, Vol 1, 4th ed., Addison-Wesley, 1986

Information processing systems – Database language SQL, OSI, 1986

Lynch, E.,*Understanding SQL*, Macmillan Education, 1990

Oracle: Set of Guides and Manuals for the Oracle DBMS, Oracle Corporation.

Index